DINING OUT AT HOME
EDMONTON

Served by Myriam Leighton & Jennifer Stead

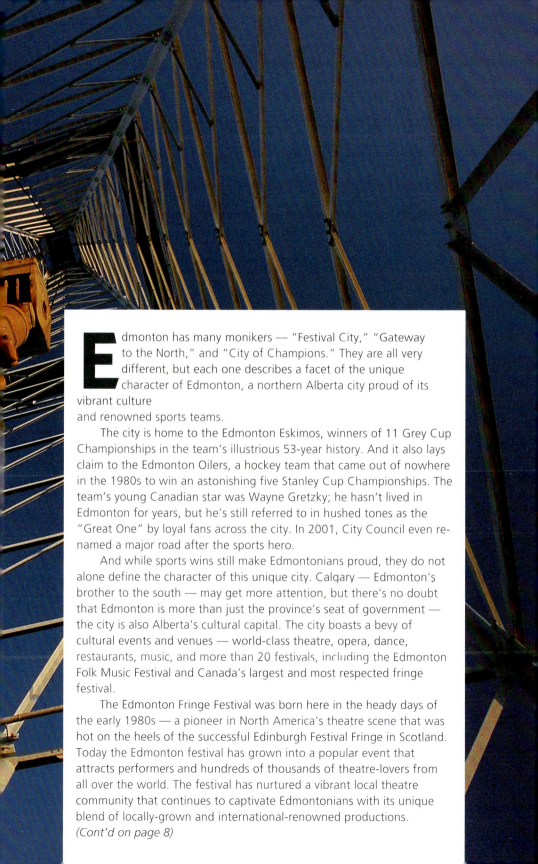

Edmonton has many monikers — "Festival City," "Gateway to the North," and "City of Champions." They are all very different, but each one describes a facet of the unique character of Edmonton, a northern Alberta city proud of its vibrant culture and renowned sports teams.

The city is home to the Edmonton Eskimos, winners of 11 Grey Cup Championships in the team's illustrious 53-year history. And it also lays claim to the Edmonton Oilers, a hockey team that came out of nowhere in the 1980s to win an astonishing five Stanley Cup Championships. The team's young Canadian star was Wayne Gretzky; he hasn't lived in Edmonton for years, but he's still referred to in hushed tones as the "Great One" by loyal fans across the city. In 2001, City Council even re-named a major road after the sports hero.

And while sports wins still make Edmontonians proud, they do not alone define the character of this unique city. Calgary — Edmonton's brother to the south — may get more attention, but there's no doubt that Edmonton is more than just the province's seat of government — the city is also Alberta's cultural capital. The city boasts a bevy of cultural events and venues — world-class theatre, opera, dance, restaurants, music, and more than 20 festivals, including the Edmonton Folk Music Festival and Canada's largest and most respected fringe festival.

The Edmonton Fringe Festival was born here in the heady days of the early 1980s — a pioneer in North America's theatre scene that was hot on the heels of the successful Edinburgh Festival Fringe in Scotland. Today the Edmonton festival has grown into a popular event that attracts performers and hundreds of thousands of theatre-lovers from all over the world. The festival has nurtured a vibrant local theatre community that continues to captivate Edmontonians with its unique blend of locally-grown and international-renowned productions.

(Cont'd on page 8)

Top: *The Edmonton skyline*

Bottom: *The Provincial Legislature Building*

Opposite top left: *Hole's Greenhouses and Gardens in St. Albert*

Opposite top right: *A view of downtown Edmonton*

Opposite bottom: *Edmonton's history is firmly rooted in western traditions.*

Top: *Inside the West Edmonton Mall*   **Bottom:** *The water park at the West Edmonton Mall.*

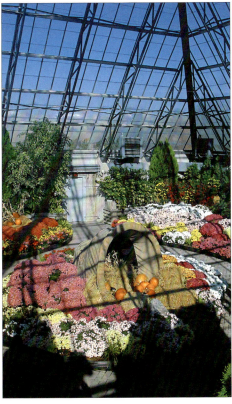

Top: Grant McEwan Hall

Bottom left: The Muttart Conservatory features more than 700 species of plants.

Bottom right: Ukrainian religion and culture are strong Edmonton historical traditions.

Left: *A girl in ethnic Ukrainian clothing*

Right: *Inside a trading store at Fort Edmonton*

(Continued from page 3)

But even as the city's denizens line up to see the latest in "edgy" theatre, they also revel in the traditions of a rich cultural past. Every summer, for example, hundreds of thousands celebrate Klondike Days, a 10-day fair named for that famous gold rush of 1898, when thousands of prospectors passed through Edmonton, following an inland route to the Yukon. Though their destination was remote, the rush through town nonetheless put Edmonton on the map, triggering an unprecedented boom that saw the population double in just two years.

Today, more than 100 years later, Edmonton is no small speck on a map. It is Alberta's second largest city and it continues to grow at a dizzying pace. The influx of new faces will no doubt be part of the evolution of the city, increasing not just Edmonton's physical size, but its multicultural heritage, sophistication, and cultural clout.

DINING OUT AT HOME
EDMONTON

Served by
Myriam Leighton & Jennifer Stead
Altitude Publishing

Altitude Publishing Canada Ltd.
The Canadian Rockies
1500 Railway Avenue
Canmore, Alberta T1W 1P6
www.altitudepublishing.com
Copyright 2003 © Myriam Leighton and Jennifer Stead

Canadian Cataloguing in Publication Data

Leighton, Myriam, 1962-
Dining out at home : Edmonton / Myriam Leighton, Jennifer Stead, editors.

(Dining Out at Home)
Includes index.
ISBN 1-55153-931-4

1. Cookery--Alberta--Edmonton. 2. Cookery, Canadian--Alberta style. I. Stead, Jennifer. II. Title. III. Series: Dining out at home. (Canmore, Alta.)
TX715.6.L45 2003   641.597123'34   C2003-9102670X

Project Development

Cover/illustrations	Jennifer Stead
Introduction	Megan Lappi
Photos	Andrew Bradley
Title page photo	Doug Leighton
Editing & Layout	Kara Turner
Food consulting	Roger McGregor

Altitude GreenTree Program

Altitude Publishing will plant in Canada twice as many trees as were used in the manufacturing of this product.

Made in Western Canada
Printed and bound in Canada by Friesen Printers, Altona, Manitoba

We acknowledge the financial support of the Government of Canada through the Book Publishing Industry Development Program (BPIDP) for our publishing activities.

Table of Contents

Preface

With **Dining Out at Home, Edmonton**, we offer you a selection of recipes from the creative chefs working in the fine restaurants of this city. These chefs, both established and new, have contributed significantly to the liveliness and diversity of Edmonton's culinary offerings and are included here for their creativity and innovation. It is in the nature of the business that restaurants and chefs reinvent themselves periodically, reflecting urban changes, personal growth, and a desire for change. Therefore we have also included recipes from a few chefs whose careers and establishments are in transition, but who have contributed to the diversity and culinary expertise in Edmonton. We hope that the collection of recipes in this book will inspire you and add some excitement to your menus while cooking in the comfort of your own home.

It has been a wonderfully interesting and instructive experience, working with so many fabulous chefs. In gathering the recipes together and presenting the creations of the various chefs we have tried to stay true to individual style and approach. The result is a mélange of meals from a wide range of restaurants sure to satisfy everyone.

We would like to thank and acknowledge all the exceptional restaurants and chefs for their time and creative generosity, our food editors, Roger McGregor and Colleen Dorion, and everyone else who made this possible.

Enjoy!

Myriam and Jennifer

Bonus! Recipe Sampler!

Additional recipes are available on the web.
Please visit **www.altitudepublishing.com**
and follow the links to
Dining Out at Home, Edmonton.

Breakfasts

Chorizo and Tomato Basil Salsa Frittata

Serves: 1

2 oz.	Chorizo sausage	55 g

Precook the Chorizo over medium heat until completely cooked through. Drain excess grease and set aside.

Salsa

1	Medium tomato, finely chopped	1
1/2 oz.	Fresh basil, chopped	15 g
1/4 cup	Olive oil	50 ml
1 tsp.	Cilantro, chopped	5 ml
dash	Tabasco sauce	a few drops
to taste	Salt and pepper	to taste

For salsa, mix tomato, basil, olive oil and cilantro together. Add Tabasco and salt and pepper to taste. Place in refrigerator for 1 hour to let flavours meld.

3	Eggs, whipped well	3
1 oz.	Asiago cheese, grated	30 g

To complete, preheat an 8-inch (20 cm) Teflon frying pan over medium high heat for about 20 seconds. Spray pan with an oil coating. Pour egg mixture into pan. Using a rubber spatula, push the outside edges towards the middle to cook evenly. When egg mixture is almost fully cooked, place salsa on top, then Chorizo, and top with Asiago cheese. Slide out of pan onto plate and enjoy.

Brian Leadbetter, Executive Chef
Madison's Grill — Union Bank Inn

Field and Forest Mushroom Melt

Serves: 1

1/2	Portobello mushroom, diced	1/2
3	Oyster mushrooms, sliced	3
4	Button mushrooms, sliced	4
1 oz.	Clarified butter	20 g
1 tbsp.	Fresh parsley, chopped	15 ml
1/4 tsp.	Garlic, minced	1 ml
1	Bagel, sliced and toasted	1
2 oz.	Boursin cheese*	50 g
1 oz.	Applewood Smoked Cheddar, sliced	20 g
to taste	Salt and pepper	to taste

Sauté mushrooms in the clarified butter for 2 minutes at a maximum temperature, then lower the heat to a moderate temperature and add the parsley and garlic. Sauté for another 2 minutes and season to taste. Toast the bagel and spread with Boursin cheese, then place the sautéed mushrooms generously on top, cover with the smoked cheddar and melt under the broiler. Serve immediately.

* Available in the deli section of most grocery stores.

Serving suggestion: Serve with hash browns and fresh fruit.

Roary MacPherson C.C.C., Executive Chef
The Fairmont Hotel Macdonald

Oatmeal and Rye Flour Saskatoon Berry Pancakes
with Chocolate Butter

Yields: 12 pancakes

Chocolate Butter

1/2 cup	Bittersweet chocolate, melted	125 ml
1/2 cup	Butter, unsalted, softened	125 ml

In small bowl, fold chocolate into butter, and set aside. Using a star-tipped piping bag, pipe 1 oz. (30 g) florets onto parchment paper and place in fridge.

Pancakes

1/2 cup	All-purpose flour	125 ml
1/2 cup	Rye flour	125 ml
1/2 cup	Rolled oats	125 ml
1/2 tsp.	Salt	2 ml
1 tbsp.	Baking powder	15 ml
1 1/4 tsp.	White sugar	6 ml
1	Egg	1
1 cup	Buttermilk	250 ml
1/2 tbsp.	Butter, melted	8 ml
1/2 cup	Frozen Saskatoon berries, thawed	125 ml

In a large bowl, sift together flour, rye flour, rolled oats, salt, baking powder, and sugar. In a small bowl, beat together egg and buttermilk. Stir milk and egg mixture into flour mixture. Mix in the butter and fold in the Saskatoon berries. Set aside for 1 hour.

Heat a lightly oiled griddle or frying pan over medium heat. Pour or scoop the batter onto the griddle, using approximately 1/4 cup (50 ml) for each pancake. Brown both sides and serve hot, with chocolate butter.

Jasmin Kobajica, Executive Chef
La Ronde, Chateau Lacombe

Appetizers, Sauces & Sides

Baked Goat Cheese
with Fresh Tomato Salad

Serves: 6

1/2 cup	Snow goat cheese	125 g
to taste	Cracked pepper	to taste
dash	Olive oil	dash
1	Baguette	1

Place a round of goat cheese in a small bowl or ramekin. Season lightly with pepper and olive oil and place under the oven broiler for 5 to 10 minutes until lightly browned.

Fresh Tomato Salad

Tomatoes, sliced
Basil, chopped
Balsamic vinegar
Olive oil

Drizzle sliced tomatoes with vinegar and oil and garnish with basil.

Serving suggestion: Serve baked cheese with a toasted, buttered baguette and fresh tomato salad.

Gordon Guiltner, Executive Chef
Café Select

Escallops Valle D'Auges

Serves: 4

2 tbsp.	Butter	30 ml
8 oz.	Veal escallops, thinly sliced across the grain	250 g
to taste	Salt and pepper	to taste
1/2 cup	Mushrooms, sliced	125 ml
1 oz.	Calvados	30 ml
1/4 cup	Cream	50 ml

Melt butter over medium heat. Add veal, season with salt and pepper. Add mushrooms and cook until semi soft. Flambé with Calvados being very careful of the flame. Finish with cream. Let it reduce.

Serving suggestion: Serve with sliced apple.

Mike Day, Chef
Three Muskateers

Alberta Beef Tataki
with Ginger and Green Onion Mashed Potato and Mixed Root Vegetable Ratatouille

Serves: 4-8

2 lbs.	Alberta striploin	1 kg

Marinade

4 tbsp.	Soya sauce	50 ml
4 tbsp.	Red wine	50 ml
2 tbsp.	Corn syrup	30 ml
to taste	Salt and pepper	to taste

Mix all of the above ingredients together and marinate striploin for at least 4 hours.

Sear it in a hot pan for 1 minute on each side or until desired temperature is reached.

Ginger and Green Onion Mashed Potato

6	Potatoes, medium	6
2 tbsp.	Fresh ginger, finely minced	30 ml
3	Green onions, finely chopped	3
2/3 cup	Whipping cream	150 ml

Peel potatoes and boil them in water until soft. Mash. Add ginger, green onion, and whipping cream, and salt and pepper to taste.

Ratatouille

2 tbsp.	Cooking oil	30 ml
1	Onion, finely minced	1
2 cups	Mixed root vegetables, diced:	500 ml
	carrot, beet, parsnip and daikon radish	
5 tbsp.	Soya sauce	65 ml
5 tbsp.	Balsamic vinegar	65 ml
6 tbsp.	Maple syrup	80 ml
1 cup	Red wine	250 ml
Garnish	Green onion and tomatoes, diced	Garnish

Place cooking oil in a hot pan, add minced onion and sauté the mixed root vegetables until al dente. In a separate saucepan mix soya sauce, balsamic vinegar, maple syrup, and red wine and reduce over medium heat to a thick solution. Season with salt and pepper to taste.

Assembly: Place the ratatouille in the centre of a plate, mashed potato on top of ratatouille and slices of beef tataki on the potato. Drizzle the reduction around the food. Garnish with slivered green onions and diced tomatoes.

Serving suggestion: Traditionally, this is served as an appetizer, but it may be served as an entrée as well.

Judy Wu, Executive Chef
Polos Café

Note:
This was the champion dish of the 1999
All Canadian Chef Race Competition.

Coquilles St. Jacques

Serves: 4

1 tbsp.	Butter	15 ml
8 oz.	Mushrooms, sliced	250 g
10 oz.	Scallops	300 g
3 oz.	Onion, chopped	75 g
1/2 cup	White wine	125 ml
2 cups	Whipping cream	500 ml
1/2 cup	Hollandaise sauce	125 ml

In a small amount of butter, sauté the mushrooms and onions until onions are clear. Add scallops and wine; simmer for 2 minutes. Remove scallops and add cream to the mushrooms. Boil together until cream thickens. Season with salt and pepper.

Pipe from a piping bag with a star tip, a ring of Duchess potatoes (see recipe below) around a soup plate or scallop shell. Add mushrooms and scallops, top with Hollandaise sauce and broil in the oven until lightly browned on top.

Duchess Potatoes

2 lbs.	Potatoes	1 kg
3 tbsp.	Butter	45 ml
1/4 cup	Milk	50 ml
2-3	Eggs	2-3

Boil cubed peeled potatoes until soft. Mash with a bit of butter, milk and eggs. Season with salt and white pepper to taste.

Gordon Guiltner, Executive Chef
Café Select

Beignets aux fromage (Cheese Fritters)

Yields: approximately 24

8 oz.	Water	250 ml
1/3 cup	Milk	75 ml
1/3 cup	White wine	75 ml
1 tsp.	Butter	5 ml

Mix all above ingredients together in a saucepan and bring to a boil.

10 oz.	Flour	300 g
6 oz.	Swiss cheese, grated	150 g
5-6	Eggs	5-6
to taste	Salt, white pepper, nutmeg	to taste

Add flour to hot liquid and cook, working hard with a wooden spoon. Remove from heat. Blend cheese into the dough. Blend the eggs into the mixture. Season to taste with salt, white pepper, and nutmeg. Heat oil to 350° F (180° C) and deep fry 1 tbsp. (15 ml) of batter or so at a time until well browned and puffed up. These are best made shortly before serving.

Serving suggestion: Serve with a flavourful tomato sauce for dipping.

Gordon Guiltner, Executive Chef
Café Select

Green Curry Butter Sauce

Yields: 1 1/2 cups (375 ml), pasta sauce for 6 servings

1/3 cup	Stock: fish, vegetable or chicken	75 ml
1 cup	Butter	250 ml
1/4 cup	Green Curry Paste mixture, (see recipe below)	50 ml
pinch	Cayenne pepper, optional	pinch

In a saucepan, bring stock and 1/2 cup (125 ml) of butter to boil. Pour boiling liquid into blender, using extreme caution when blending hot liquids. Add remaining 1/2 cup (125 ml) of butter and 1/4 cup (50 ml) green curry paste and blend. Adjust flavour to your taste with salt, pepper, curry powder and/or cayenne. If you need the sauce thicker or thinner, increase or decrease the amount of stock.

Green Curry Mixture

6	Garlic cloves	6
1 cup	Flat leaf parsley, washed, spun dry	250 ml
1 cup	Fresh cilantro, washed, spun dry	250 ml
1/2 cup	Fresh spinach, washed, spun dry, stems removed	125 ml
1 tsp.	Thai Green curry paste*	5 ml
1 tsp.	Curry powder	5 ml
1/2 tsp.	Salt	2 ml
1/3 cup	Canola oil	75 ml
1/3 cup	Ice water	75 ml

Wrap garlic in tinfoil and bake about 45 minutes at 350° F (180° C). May be stored in the fridge for up to 4 days. Blend all ingredients in blender on high, until smooth. This paste can be frozen for future use. *Thai Green curry paste is available in Asian markets and often in local grocery stores.

Serving suggestions: This sauce is a fresh-tasting sauce that enhances the flavours of any simply prepared fish or chicken, or toss with pasta and sautéed vegetables and serve with a salad.

Darcy Radies, Chef
The Blue Pear

Choma Choma

Serves: 2

1 lb.	Beef ribs	500 g
2 tsp.	Red chilli powder	10 ml
1 tsp.	Salt	5 ml
1/2 tsp.	Citric acid powder	2 ml
	Oil for brushing	

Precook ribs by boiling them for 15 minutes in a large pot of water. Mix chilli, salt and citric acid powder together. Place beef ribs onto the grill. Brush the ribs with oil and sprinkle half the chilli mixture onto the ribs. Cook for 3 to 4 minutes. Turn them over, sprinkle the rest of the chilli mixture on them and cook another 3 to 4 minutes. Slice and serve on a platter.

Victor D'Alves, Director
Khazana Restaurant

Chicken Liver Pâté

Serves: 2

1 tsp.	Fresh garlic, minced	5 ml
1	Small onion, diced	1
2 tbsp.	Brandy	30 ml
2 tbsp.	Marsala	30 ml
2 tsp.	Worcestershire sauce	10 ml
1 tbsp.	White sugar	15 ml
1/3 cup	White wine	75 ml
pinch each	Basil, thyme and oregano	pinch each
dash	Tabasco	dash
pinch	Salt and pepper	pinch
12 oz.	Chicken livers	350 g
2 tsp.	Dijon mustard	10 ml
2 tsp.	Tomato paste	10 ml
1/2 lb.	Melted butter	250 g

To make the reduction, simmer together garlic, onion, brandy, Marsala, Worcestershire sauce, sugar, white wine, basil, thyme, oregano and Tabasco. Reduce by half, then strain and cool. Reserve liquid only. Purée livers with Dijon mustard and tomato paste in a blender or food processor. Combine liver mixture in a bowl with butter and the reduction, and mix thoroughly. Press liver mixture through a strainer. Pour equal amounts into two, 3-inch (7.5 cm) diameter, flat-bottomed glass bowls or ramekins. Cook in a water-bath at 375° F (190° C) for 40 to 45 minutes. Let chill and release from the bowls with a knife.

Serving suggestion: Serve with sliced French bread.

Cui Kouch, Chef de cuisine
Normand's

Polenta Crackers

Yields: Approximately 24 crackers

1 cup	All purpose flour	250 ml
3/4 cup	Polenta	175 ml
1/2 cup	Semolina	125 ml
1 tsp.	Salt	5 ml
1 cup	Milk	250 ml
1 tsp.	Olive oil	5 ml

Combine the first four ingredients. Add milk and olive oil. Combine together to make a dough, kneading up to 5 to 10 minutes. If the dough is too wet, add more flour until the dough is no longer sticky. Let dough rest for 1 hour.

Preheat oven to 350° F (180° C).

Cut the dough into six even pieces. Roll out each piece as thin as possible. Bake 2 to 3 minutes or until golden brown.

Serving suggestion: Serve with a cheese platter.

Patrizio Sacchetto, Master Chef
Via Vai

Atlantic Salmon Tartar

Serves: 4

12 oz.	Fresh Atlantic salmon, skinned and de-boned	350 g
1/2 cup	Purple onion, finely diced	125 ml
1 tbsp.	Capers, finely diced	15 ml
1 tbsp.	Grainy Dijon mustard	15 ml
2 tsp.	Lemon zest, minced	10 ml
2 tsp.	Garlic, roasted	10 ml
2 tsp.	Extra virgin olive oil	10 ml
to taste	Salt and pepper	to taste

Finely dice fresh salmon and place into a mixing bowl. Add onion, capers, Dijon, lemon zest and garlic to the salmon. Gently toss together all the ingredients with the olive oil and season with salt and pepper.

Serving suggestion: Serve with fresh rye bread or multigrain baguette.

Darrell Russell, Pastry Chef
Café de Ville

Corn Bread

Makes one 9 x 13 inch (22 x 32 cm) loaf

1 1/2 cups	Diced onion	375 ml
1 tbsp.	Vegetable oil	15 ml
3 cups	Cheddar cheese, shredded	750 ml
2 1/4 cups	Corn meal	625 ml
3 cups	All purpose flour	750 ml
3 cups	Corn niblets	750 ml
3 cups	Milk	750 ml
3	Eggs	3
3/4 cup	Vegetable oil	175 ml
6 oz.	Honey	170 g
1 tsp.	Salt	5 ml
3 tbsp.	Baking powder	45 ml

Sauté onion in 1 tbsp. (15ml) oil for 5 minutes. Mix half of the cheese with remaining ingredients. Pour into a greased 9 x 13 inch (22 x 32cm) baking pan and top with the other half of cheese. Bake in a preheated 350° F (180° C) oven for 45 minutes.

Chuck Phillips, Owner/Chef
Highlevel Diner

Rare Ahi Tuna
Spring Rolls

Yields: 12 rolls

16 oz.	Fresh Ahi tuna, thumb size pieces	500 g
to taste	Wasabi paste	to taste
to taste	Fresh cilantro, chopped	to taste
12	Spring roll wrappers, 6 inch (15 cm) square	12
1	Whole egg, beaten	1

Lay out wrappers diagonally. Brush with egg along all sides. Place a piece of tuna in centre of each wrapper, top with Wasabi paste and chopped cilantro. Starting at the bottom corner, roll up the wrapper and fold in the sides as you go. Deep-fry until golden brown, approximately 1 to 2 minutes and slice in half.

Serving suggestion: Serve with a light soy sauce or Ponzu sauce for dipping.

Substitute: For those concerned about dwindling numbers of wild tuna, salmon can be substituted for the tuna in this recipe.

Donna Rumboldt, Chef/Owner
Donna at the Citadel

Cucumber Avocado Mayo

Yields: 3 cups (750 ml)

1/2	Cucumber, de-seeded	1/2
2 cups	Mayonnaise	500 ml
1/2 cup	Sour cream	125 ml
2	Avocados	2
1/2	Lemon, juiced	1/2
1	Scallion, finely chopped	1
1/4 cup	Fresh parsley, finely chopped	50 ml

Grate cucumber and set aside to drain. Stir mayonnaise and sour cream together. Mash avocados with lemon juice and blend with mayonnaise mixture. Add scallions, parsley and drained cucumber and stir well.

Serving suggestion: Makes a great addition to meat sandwiches, such as BBQ pork, or in vegetarian sandwiches. Can also be used as a dip for vegetables, or as an accompaniment for cold poached fish such as salmon or halibut.

Ross Munro, Executive Chef
Pradera Café and Lounge, The Westin

Curried Maple Mango Sauce

Yields: 4 cups (1 litre)

2 oz.	Curry powder	55 g
2 cups	Mango purée	500 ml
2 cups	Pure maple syrup	500 ml
to taste	Salt and white pepper	to taste
1/4 cup	Champagne vinegar	60 ml

Toast the curry powder in a dry frying pan. After it turns a nice golden brown, remove from heat and add mango purée. Place back on heat and stir in the maple syrup. Season with salt and pepper to taste. Add the champagne vinegar and remove from heat. Let chill in refrigerator for at least 2 hours.

Serving suggestion: Use as dipping sauce for chicken wings, with meat fondue, or as a glaze for salmon or shrimp.

Ross Munro, Executive Chef
Pradera Café and Lounge, The Westin

Ermite Bleu Vinaigrette

Yields: 2 cups (500 ml)

3 oz.	Ermite Bleu cheese, such as St. Benoit, Quebec, crumbled	85 g
1/4 cup	Red wine vinegar	50 ml
1/4 cup	White vinegar	50 ml
1/4	Red onion	1/4
few leaves	Fresh basil, chopped	few leaves
1 1/2 tsp.	Worcestershire sauce	7 ml
3 stems	Fresh chives	3 stems
1	Shallot	1
2 tsp.	Dijon mustard	10 ml
1 1/2 cups	Olive oil	375 ml
to taste	Salt and white pepper	to taste

Break cheese into small pieces and mix all ingredients well. Refrigerate.

Serving suggestion: Great for fresh green salads, dipping freshly grilled pieces of French baguette, or as a sauce for chicken wings.

Ross Munro, Executive Chef
Pradera Café and Lounge, The Westin

Mushroom Ragout

Serves: 12

1/4 cup	Butter	50 ml
4 cups	Sliced mushrooms, such as button, oyster or shitake mushrooms	1 litre
1/4 cup	Leeks, diced	50 ml
1 tbsp.	Garlic, roasted	15 ml
2 tbsp.	Fresh chopped herbs, such as basil, rosemary, and dill	30 ml
to taste	Salt and pepper	to taste
1/4 cup	Red wine	50 ml
1 1/2 cups	Demi-glaze	375 ml
1/2 cup	Whipping cream	125 ml
2 cups	Feta cheese, for garnish	500 ml

In a sauce pot, melt butter over a medium heat. Add mushrooms, leeks, garlic, herbs, and salt and pepper and sauté until mushrooms become soft. Deglaze with red wine, add demi-glaze and whipping cream. Bring to a simmer and reduce ragout until slightly thickened.

Serving suggestion: Serve with polenta soufflé (opposite). Top each piece of soufflé with some ragout and sprinkle with crumbled Feta cheese.

Paul Campbell, Executive Chef
Café de Ville

Polenta Soufflé

Serves: 12

12	Eggs	12
1/2 cup	Whipping cream	125 ml
10 oz.	Spinach, sautéed	300 g
2 tbsp.	Garlic, chopped	30 ml
2 tbsp.	Fresh chopped herbs, such as basil, rosemary, or dill	30 ml
3 cups	Parmesan or Sprinz, grated	750 ml
1 1/2 cups	Stilton, crumbled	375 ml
to taste	Salt and pepper	to taste
3 cups	Half and half cream	750 ml
3 cups	Milk	750 ml
1 cup	Cornmeal	250 ml

Preheat oven to 300° F (150° C) and line bottom and sides of a 10-inch (25 cm) spring-form pan with parchment paper. In a large bowl mix eggs, whipping cream, spinach, garlic, herbs, Parmesan, Stilton, salt and pepper. In a medium pot bring half and half cream with milk to a simmer. Whisk in cornmeal and cook until the mixture begins to thicken. Remove from heat and mix with the egg mixture. Pour into lined spring-form pan and bake at 300° F (150° C) for 90 minutes. Remove the ring from the spring form pan and cut into 12 slices.

Serving suggestion: Serve with mushroom ragout (opposite).

Paul Campbell, Executive Chef
Café de Ville

Phyllo Wrapped
Thai Prawns and Brie
with Sambuca Espresso Bean Cream

Serves: 12

1 pack	Phyllo pastry sheets	1 pack
1 cup	Butter, melted	250 ml
12	Brie, 2-inch (50 mm) squares	12
12	Tiger prawns, 26/30 count	12

Place phyllo on counter (work quickly so pastry does not dry out), brush one layer with melted butter and place second layer over top; butter again. Cut buttered phyllo lengthwise into vertical strips, 3 1/2 inches (8 cm) wide. Do this until there are 12 strips (it may be easier to do this in 3 sets of 4 strips rather than 12 at once). Place a square of Brie at the bottom of each strip with a prawn on top of the Brie. Carefully fold cheese, prawn and pastry over and towards left hand edge of pastry then fold corner at bottom left up towards the top of the strip. Repeat this folding and rolling motion until strip is used and a triangle is formed. Brush the outside with melted butter. Repeat until there are 12 triangles. Refrigerate until triangles are firm. Bake in a preheated oven at 350° F (180° C) for 4 to 6 minutes or until golden brown. Serve with Sambuca Cream.

Sambuca Espresso Bean Cream

3 1/2 cups	Heavy cream	800 ml
6 tbsp.	Espresso beans	90 ml
3 oz.	Sambuca	85 ml

Combine cream and espresso beans in a saucepan on medium high heat. Reduce cream by half, whisking constantly. Strain, add Sambuca and simmer until all alcohol is cooked out.

Serving suggestion: Lorraine Ellis and Sabrina Warnholz, our wine stewards, recommend quite a dry white wine such as Australia's Jacob's Creek Semillion-Chardonnay.

Chris Davies, Chef
Manor Café

Spätzle

Serves: 4

1 cup	Milk	200 ml
1 cup	Water	200 ml
2	Eggs	2
1 lb.	All purpose flour (about 4 cups)	450 g
to taste	Salt	to taste
pinch	White pepper	pinch
pinch	Nutmeg	pinch
	Butter for frying	

Mix first four ingredients together and beat until slightly elastic, but not tough. Then add seasoning. Press batter through a food mill with 1/4 inch (6 mm) holes, or a colander with large holes, directly into a pot of boiling water. If making larger quantities, process in batches. Blanch until spätzle swim on top, remove with slotted spoon, cool off in cold water, drain and drip dry.

For service, melt butter in frying pan over medium heat, add spätzle and fry lightly. Adjust seasoning with salt and pepper.

Serving suggestion: Serve as is or mix with a white sauce, top with cheese and gratin in preheated oven until golden brown.

Note: Can be made ahead and stored in refrigerator for up to 3 days. Spätzle sieves are available in specialty kitchen stores.

Peter Johner, Chef/Owner
Packrat Louie Kitchen & Bar

Roast Tomato Tart

Serves: 4

4	Puff pastry, cut into small circles	4
2	Tomatoes	2
4	Garlic cloves, sliced	4
2 leaves	Basil, fresh	2 leaves
1/4 cup	Olive oil	50 ml
1/8 cup	Balsamic vinegar	25 ml
to taste	Salt and pepper	to taste
to taste	Black pepper, cracked	to taste
4 tbsp.	Feta cheese	60 ml

Bake puff pastry circles for about 15 minutes or according to package directions and let cool. Blanch the tomatoes for about 12 seconds in boiling water, then put them in ice water to cool. Peel, cut in half and take out the seeds. Toss tomatoes with garlic, basil, olive oil, balsamic vinegar, salt and pepper. Place on a pan and roast for about 12 minutes at 300-325° F (150-165° C).

Fill tomato halves with crumbled Feta cheese and place a circle of pastry on top of each tomato half then flip over carefully to avoid cheese falling out.

Sauce

1/4 cup	Red wine	50 m
3 tbsp.	Balsamic vinegar	45 ml
2 oz.	Butter	60 g

Reduce red wine, add a touch of balsamic vinegar and stir in butter. Pour over tart.

Serving suggestion: Garnish with basil, pearl onions and more Feta cheese.

Shonn Oborowsky, Executive Chef
Characters

Rock Shrimp Cakes

Yields: 12-15 cakes

1 cup	Red pepper	250 ml
1 cup	Celery	250 ml
small can	Water chestnuts	small can
1	Yellow onion, medium	1
1/4 tsp.	Dried parsley	1 ml
1/4 cup	Lemongrass	50 ml
3	Garlic, cloves	3
1/4 cup	Ginger	50 ml
24 oz.	Rock shrimp or lobster	750 g

Chop all ingredients except Rock shrimp or lobster finely in a food processor. Mix all ingredients together; form into cakes using a ring mould. Chill to set for several hours or overnight.

1 cup	Flour	250 ml
3	Eggs	3
1 cup	Panko breadcrumbs	250 ml
to taste	Salt	to taste

To cook, dip cakes in flour then in egg, then in Panko breadcrumbs and sprinkle with some salt. Deep fry at 350° F (180° C) until golden brown.

Substitute: If you don't have Panko bread crumbs use any coarse soft breadcrumbs.

Serving suggestion: Serve with a sauce like Ponzu, Hoisin or chili sauce.

Donna Rumboldt, Chef/Owner
Donna at the Citadel

Grilled Vegetable Terrine

Yields: 24 slices

1 1/2 cups	Olive oil	375 ml
3/4 cup	Balsamic vinegar	175 ml
to taste	Coarse salt	to taste
to taste	Pepper	to taste
1	Lemon, juiced	1
3	Eggplants, large	3
1	Zucchini, large	1
1	Yellow squash, large	1
3	Red peppers	3
3	Yellow peppers	3
2	Leeks	2
2 1/2 tbsp.	Unflavoured gelatin	40 ml
4 cups	Vegetable stock	1 litre
1 1/4 cup	Aspic	300 ml
1 tsp.	Fresh parsley, minced	5 ml
1 tsp.	Fresh thyme, minced	5 ml
1 tsp.	Fresh chives, minced	5 ml

Combine olive oil, vinegar, salt and pepper to taste. Set aside. Wash, remove blemishes and trim stem ends of eggplant, zucchini and squash. Cut lengthwise into 1/4 inch (0.5 cm) thick slices, discarding end pieces. You will need 10 slices of eggplant and 5 slices each of zucchini and squash. Place vegetables in a shallow dish and pour 1/2 cup (125 ml) of olive oil mixture over them. Toss and marinate for 1 hour.

Preheat grill or broiler. Place whole peppers on a hot grill or under broiler. Turn frequently for about 5 minutes or until skins have blackened. Remove and place in a container to cool for 5 minutes or until skins can be brushed off easily. Remove and discard the skins. Carefully split peppers open. Remove and discard stems, seeds and membrane. Lay the peppers interior side down on a paper towel to drain. Reserve each colour separately.
Preheat oven to 350° F (180° C).

Grill marinated vegetables on the grill or under the broiler for 4 minutes, turning often until cooked but not mushy. Place in a shallow container, toss with 1/4 cup (50 ml) of olive oil mixture and set aside.

Trim leeks of all green parts, roots and any tough outer leaves. Wash them several times in cold water. Cut lengthwise into the centre but not right through the leeks. Rinse under water again. Open leeks into butterflies and place in steamer. Cover and steam for 10 to 12 minutes or until tender. Drain on paper towel. Set aside.

Combine gelatin with one cup of stock in a small saucepan and allow to sit for 2 minutes to soften. Place the pan over low heat and stir for 1 minute or until dissolved. Heat the remaining 3 cups of stock in a medium saucepan over medium heat until just warmed. Whisk in softened gelatin stirring until blended. Season to taste with salt and pepper and let cool to room temperature. When cool, stir in the herbs. Place about 2 tbsp. (30 ml) of the herbed aspic in a very small container in an ice bath for a few minutes. Then test for consistency and seasoning. It should be soft and slightly firm, but not thick like Jell-O.

Spray a 12 x 4 x 4 inch (30 x 10 x 10 cm) terrine with non-stick vegetable oil. Carefully line it with plastic wrap allowing a 2-3 inch (5-8 cm) overhang all around. Pour 1/4 cup (50 ml) of aspic into the bottom. Pour 1 cup (250 ml) of aspic into a large mixing bowl to use for dipping. One at a time, dip eggplant slices into the aspic and place in the terrine. Put 2 slices of eggplant on the bottom to cover it and 4 along each long side, slightly overlapping each other. They should over hang the top edge by about 2 inches (5 cm). Pour in a layer of aspic and season with salt and pepper. Add a layer of yellow squash, then zucchini, dipping each slice in aspic and seasoning each layer. Push down on layers and add aspic as needed. Gently pull leeks apart. Dip each piece into aspic and place in a double layer. Push down, season and add aspic if necessary to cover. Dipping each piece into the aspic as you go, layer alternating red and yellow pepper pieces. Push down, season, add aspic as needed. Finally, push down to force out any air pockets and allow aspic to fill in any holes. Fold eggplant up and over the top, seasoning and adding aspic, if necessary. Fold the plastic film over the top to cover tightly. Cut a small vent on top and give a final push to expel air. Place in the refrigerator for 8 hours to allow flavours to blend and aspic to set. When ready to serve, lift it from the terrine and slice it cross wise into 1/2 inch (1 cm) thick slices.

Patrizio Sacchetto, Master Chef
Via Vai

Avocado Cocktail

Serves: 2

| 1 | Avocado, ripe | 1 |
| 2 cups | Baby shrimp, cooked | 500 ml |

Cocktail sauce

1	Egg yolk	1
1 tsp.	Dijon mustard	5 ml
to taste	Salt and pepper	to taste
1/2 cup	Vegetable oil	125 ml
1/2 cup	Ketchup	125 ml
1 tsp.	Tabasco sauce	5 ml
1 tsp.	Worcestershire sauce	5 ml
1 tbsp.	Brandy	15 ml
1 tsp.	Lemon juice	5 ml

In a medium-sized bowl or a food processor, mix egg yolk, mustard, salt and pepper. Slowly start whisking and drizzle oil into mixture until desired mayonnaise consistency is achieved. Stir the remaining ingredients into the sauce. Cut avocado in half and remove the pit. Using a spoon, carefully scoop the avocado out of the shell keeping the shell and the avocado half intact. Thinly slice the avocado halves and fan out onto plates. Pour shrimp and sauce into the avocado shells.

Serving suggestion: Serve with a garnish of lettuce and a slice of lemon.

Mike Day, Chef
Three Muskateers

Soups
& Salads

Mulligatawny

Serves: 4-6

1/2 cup	Cooking oil	125 ml
1/3 cup	Celery, diced	75 ml
1/2 tsp.	Garlic, minced	2 ml
1/3 cup	Onion, diced	75 ml
1/3 cup	Carrot, diced	75 ml
1 tbsp.	Curry powder	15 ml
1/2 tbsp.	Cumin	7 ml
1/8 cup	Flour	25 ml
4 cups	Chicken stock	1 litre
1/2 cup	Cream	125 ml
1/2 cup	Cooked chicken, diced	125 ml
1/2 cup	Fresh apple, diced	125 ml
1/3 cup	Cooked rice	75 ml
to taste	Salt and pepper	to taste

Heat large stock pot with oil. Sauté celery, garlic, onion and carrot. Add curry, cumin and flour and mix well. Add the chicken stock to the mixture. Stir until it thickens slightly. Gradually add cream, seasoning, chicken, apple and rice. Bring to a boil and serve.

Chee Chu, Chef
Turtle Creek Café

Mulligatawny Soup

Serves: 2

4 oz.	Yellow lentils	100 g
1 tsp.	Salt	5 ml
1 tbsp.	Boiled rice	15 ml
1 slice	Apple	1 slice
1/2 tsp.	Cumin powder	2 ml
3/4 tsp.	Ginger paste	3 ml
1 tsp.	Lemon juice	5 ml
1 pinch	Black pepper	1 pinch
2 cups	Water	500 ml
2	Lemon wedges	2

Mix first eight ingredients together in a saucepan, add 2 cups of water and bring to a boil. When lentils are softened, blend ingredients together and serve with a lemon wedge.

Victor D'Alves, Director
Khazana Restaurant

Warm Raspberry Chicken Salad

Serves: 6

6 x 6 oz.	Chicken breasts	6 x 170 g
2 cups	Wild raspberry juice	500 ml
1/3 cup	Sugar	75 ml
1 1/4 cup	Red wine vinegar	300 ml
1 tbsp.	Dried basil	15 ml
1 tbsp.	Cornstarch	15 ml
	Toasted almonds	
	Fresh raspberries	
	Mixed greens	

Grill chicken breasts until just cooked, then julienne. In a bowl whisk together juice, sugar, and vinegar until dissolved. Stir in basil. Pour liquid into a saucepan with the grilled chicken and heat to a boil. Mix cornstarch with 2 tbsp. (30 ml) of cold water and add to the chicken mixture. Continue to heat until it has a sauce-like consistency. Place chicken over a plate of mixed greens and top with toasted almonds and fresh raspberries.

Carole DeAngelis
Carole's Café and Frank's Place

Radicchio Corsi

Serves: 4

6	Bocconcini (fresh Mozzarella balls)	6
12	Prosciutto, slices	12
1	Radiccio head	1
to taste	Salt and pepper	to taste
to taste	Shaved Parmesan	to taste
	Olive oil	
	Mixed greens	

Slice Bocconcini in half and season with salt and pepper. Wrap cheese with Prosciutto, then wrap with a radicchio leaf to make a roll. Drizzle with olive oil and cook over a hot grill until the cheese softens slightly. Finish with a drizzle of vinaigrette. Serve three per person with some mixed greens and shaved Parmesan.

Vinaigrette

1	Shallot, diced	1
1/4 cup	Red wine vinegar	50 ml
1/4 cup	Sour cherry syrup	50 ml
1/4 cup	Sun dried cherries	50 ml

Mix together and stir well.

Kevin Lendrum, Executive Chef
Il Portico

Marinated Root Vegetable Salad

Adjust quantities to your liking

Turnips
Carrots
Parsnips
Lo Bok
Celeriac
Salt and sugar
Apple cider vinegar
Salad greens
Olive oil, cold pressed
Fresh ground pepper

Wash and peel the vegetables and slice very thinly. Mix with some salt, a little sugar and apple cider vinegar.

Let stand covered overnight. Drain and arrange on some green leaves, sprinkle with cold pressed olive oil, fresh ground pepper and your favourite herb.

Peter Johner, Chef/Owner
Packrat Louie Kitchen & Bar

Polk Salad
with Sun-Dried Tomato Raspberry Vinaigrette

Serves: 2

2 cups	Spring greens, mixed	500 ml
1/2 cup	Red pepper, thinly sliced	125 ml
1/4 cup	Red onion, thinly sliced	50 ml
2	Tomatoes, quartered	2

Toss together in a bowl.

Sun-Dried Tomato Raspberry Vinaigrette

1/4 cup	Sun-dried tomatoes	50 ml
1 cup	Water	250 ml
1/4 cup	Raspberry vinegar	50 ml
2 tbsp.	Sugar	30 ml
pinch	Salt	pinch
1/2 cup	Olive oil	125 ml
1/2 cup	Raspberries, fresh or frozen	125 ml

Reconstitute sun-dried tomatoes by boiling in 1 cup (250 ml) of water for 3 to 5 minutes.

In a blender purée tomatoes briefly, then add raspberry vinegar, sugar and salt. Drizzle oil in slowly to make an emulsified mixture. Pour into a bowl and mix in raspberries.

Garnish

1/4 cup	Feta cheese	50 ml

Toss vinaigrette over tossed greens and vegetables. Garnish with crumbled feta.

Russ Paranich, Sous-Chef
Louisiana Purchase Restaurant

Chinese Cioppino

Serves: 6

2 tbsp.	Cooking oil	30 ml
4 tbsp.	Shallot, chopped	60 ml
3 tbsp.	Fresh ginger, minced	45 ml
1 tsp.	Garlic, minced	5 ml
2	Lime leaves	2
1 cup	Red wine	250 ml
2 lb.	Tomato, peeled, seeded, diced	1 kg
10 oz.	Tomato juice	300 ml
2 cups	Chicken stock	500 ml
1 lb.	Mussels	500 g
1/2 lb.	Cod fish	250 g
10 oz.	Scallops	300 g
10 oz.	Shrimps	300 g
3 tbsp.	Cilantro, chopped	45 ml
3 tbsp.	Scallions, chopped	45 ml
3 tbsp.	Shiso*, chopped	45 ml
1 tsp. each	Salt and sugar	5 ml each
to taste	Pepper	to taste
2	Eggs, beaten	2
2 oz.	Rice vermicelli	55 g

Heat cooking oil in a stock pot and sauté shallot, ginger, garlic, and lime leaves. Add red wine and reduce volume by half. Add tomato, tomato juice and chicken stock; simmer for 15 to 20 minutes. Soak rice vermicelli noodles in cool water for 20 minutes and boil in hot water for 1 minute. Drain the noodles and fry in a hot pan until they are a light-golden brown. Set aside. Add mussels and cod fish to the soup; cover and bring to a boil. Boil for 2 minutes then add the remaining seafood. Add cilantro, scallions and shiso. Add salt, sugar and pepper to taste. Add beaten eggs slowly before removing the soup from the stove. Serve and garnish with noodles. The fish and shrimp can be grilled before added to the broth for additional flavour. *Fresh basil can be used instead of Shiso.

Judy Wu, Executive Chef
Polos Café

Spinach Salad

Serves: 4-6

12 oz.	Spinach, cleaned and trimmed	350 g
3 oz.	Mushrooms	85 g
2	Oranges, cut into sections	2
1/2 cup	Onions, diced and sautéed	125 ml
3 oz.	Bacon bits	85 g
1	Hard boiled egg, sliced	1

Dressing

1/2 cup	Olive oil	125 ml
2 tbsp.	Vinegar	30 ml
1/3 cup	Orange juice	75 ml
1 tbsp.	Dill weed	15 ml
to taste	Salt and pepper	to taste

Toss all ingredients for spinach salad except for egg. Combine all dressing ingredients, toss with salad and arrange egg on top to garnish.

Chuck Phillips, Owner/Chef
Highlevel Diner

Sauerkraut Soup

Serves: 8

2	Soup bones, beef	2
4	Bay leaves	4
1 tbsp.	Ground garlic	15 ml
4 cups	Sauerkraut	1 litre
1/2 cup	Carrots, diced	125 ml
1/2 cup	Onions, diced	125 ml
1/2 cup	Potatoes, diced	125 ml
1/2 cup	Sliced cabbage	125 ml
1/2 cup	Yellow split peas	125 ml
2 tsp.	Salt	10 ml
2 tsp.	Pepper	10 ml
3 tbsp.	Margarine	45 ml
3 tbsp.	Flour	45 ml

Place soup bones in a large kettle, cover with water and cook for 15 minutes. Add bay leaves and garlic and cook for 15 minutes. Add sauerkraut and other ingredients and cook until tender. Remove the soup from the stove. Remove bones. Add salt and pepper to taste. To thicken, put flour and margarine in frying pan, cook until it forms a paste, then stir into soup and heat until it thickens. The soup can be frozen for future use.

Marge Choma, Chef/Owner
The Pyrogy House, The Pyrogy House Cook Book

Lobster and Crab Salad

Serves: 4

Lobster and Crab Mixture

1/4 cup	Mayonnaise	50 ml
2 tbsp.	Sour cream	30 g
1 tbsp.	Lemon juice	15 ml
1/4 oz.	Cilantro, chopped	7 g
2 tbsp.	Red onion, finely diced	30 ml
1/4 cup	Fresh parsley, finely chopped	50 ml
1/4	Red bell pepper, diced	1/4
1/4	Yellow bell pepper, diced	1/4
1	Scallion, finely chopped	1
2 stems	Chives, chopped	2 stems
to taste	Salt and white pepper	to taste
8 oz.	Crab claw meat	250 g
16 oz.	Frozen lobster meat, thawed	500 g

Stir mayonnaise, sour cream and lemon juice together until well blended. Then add chopped herbs, vegetables and broken-up crab and lobster meat until well coated.

2	Belgian endive, heads	2
1 tbsp.	Lemon aioli	15 ml
4	Pommes gaufrette*	4
4 oz.	Watercress	120 g
4 tbsp.	Balsamic reduction	60 ml
4 tsp.	Tumeric oil	20 ml
4 tsp.	Salmon caviar	20 ml

Assembly: Carefully spoon lobster and crab mixture onto Belgian endive leaves and form a circle. Place pomme gaufrette (*potato sliced with mandoline in criss-cross pattern and fried) in centre and top with a dollop of lemon aioli. Sprinkle the salmon caviar on top of aioli. Garnish with watercress. Now drizzle 1 tbsp. (15 ml) of balsamic reduction and 1 tsp. (5 ml) of tumeric oil over each salad plate. Enjoy.

Ross Munro, Executive Chef
Pradera Café and Lounge, The Westin

Harvest Room Spinach Salad
with Black Mustard Seed Dressing

Per serving

3 1/2 oz.	Spinach, cleaned and trimmed	100 g
2 tbsp.	Black mustard seed dressing	30 ml
to taste	Red onion, sliced	to taste
1 oz.	Shaved Oka cheese	30 g
1/4	Portobello mushroom, grilled and still warm	1/4
1/3 oz.	Sundried cranberries	10 g
	Chives and fresh herbs, for garnish	

Just before serving, toss spinach with dressing, sliced onions and some sundried cranberries.

Serving suggestion: Arrange in centre of salad plate. Top with shaved Oka, sliced Portobello mushroom, more cranberries and garnish with some chives and chopped fresh herbs.

Black Mustard Seed Dressing

Yields: 2 1/2 cups (600 ml)

1/4 cup	Black mustard seeds	50 ml
2	Egg yolks	2
1/2 cup	Olive oil	125 ml
1/2 cup	Canola oil	125 ml
1/4 cup	Champagne vinegar	50 ml
2 tbsp.	Honey	30 ml
1/2 tbsp.	Dijon mustard	7 ml
1/4 tsp.	Shallots, chopped	1 ml
1/4 tsp.	Garlic, chopped	1 ml
to taste	Salt and pepper	to taste

Cover black mustard seeds with warm water and place in refrigerator over night.

In food processor place egg yolks, olive oil, canola oil, champagne vinegar, honey and Dijon mustard. Blend until smooth, the texture of mayonnaise.

Drain water off mustard seeds and fold into dressing with shallots and garlic. Adjust seasoning.

Substitute: You can use any type of mustard.

Roary MacPherson C.C.C., Executive Chef
The Fairmont Hotel Macdonald

Butternut Squash and Ginger Soup

Serves: 12-16

1 tbsp.	Cooking oil	15 ml
1 cup	Onion, 1/4 inch (5mm) dice	250 ml
1 cup	Celery, 1/4 inch (5mm) dice	250 ml
6 cups	Butternut squash, cut into 1-inch (25mm) cubes	1.4 litres
2 tbsp.	Salt	30 ml
1 tbsp.	Pepper	15 ml
4 tbsp.	Fresh ginger, grated	60 ml
2 qts.	Chicken stock	2 litres
1/4 cup	Butter	50 ml
1/4 cup	Flour	50 ml
1 1/2 cups	Whipping cream	375 ml
	Fresh sage for garnish	
	Pear or apple slices for garnish	

In a large 1 gallon (4 litres) soup pot, cook onions and celery on low to medium heat until vegetables are soft. Add squash, salt, pepper, ginger and stock. Simmer covered, for 30 to 40 minutes, until squash is soft. In a separate pot, melt butter and add flour to make roux. Add roux to soup and whisk well. Simmer for 15 to 20 minutes. With a potato masher, mash soup and strain through a conical wire strainer. Add cream and test for flavour. Garnish with fresh sage and either pears or apples.

Serving suggestion: We recommended a Riesling or Gewürztraminer wine to accompany this dish.

Larry Stewart C.C.C., Co-owner/Chef
Hardware Grill

Oriental Summer Salad

Serves: 8

20 oz.	Boneless, skinless chicken breast	600 g

Soya Vinaigrette

6 tbsp.	Soya sauce	80 ml
3/4 cup	Red wine vinegar	175 ml
1 1/2 cups	Canola oil	375 ml
1/3 cup	Sugar	75 ml
1 oz.	Honey	30 g
1 1/2 tsp.	Fresh ginger	8 ml

Blend ingredients for the vinaigrette. Pour half of the vinaigrette over the chicken and marinate in the refrigerator for 20 minutes. Reserve leftover vinaigrette for dressing. Remove chicken and discard marinade. Cook chicken breast on the BBQ or in the oven 350° F (180° C) for 15 minutes.

4	Butter lettuce heads	4
1	Red pepper, julienned	1
1	Green pepper, julienned	1
1 cup	Bean sprouts	250 ml
2	Tomatoes, cut into wedges	2
2 tbsp.	Sesame seeds	30 ml

Clean lettuce and arrange on a plate. Place tomato wedges around the lettuce. Slice cooked chicken and place on top of lettuce. Top with julienne peppers and sprouts and sprinkle with sesame seeds. Stir dressing and pour over salad as desired. The chicken can be prepared ahead of time and kept refrigerated.

Cui Kouch, Chef de cuisine
Normand's

Roasted Sweet Potato and Red Pepper Purée
with Ovenhead Smoked Salmon Crisps

Serves 6

Roasted Sweet Potato and Red Pepper Purée

3 oz.	Canola oil	85 g
1	Large sweet potato, peeled	1
3 oz.	Onion, finely chopped	85 g
2	Red peppers, seeded	2
2	Garlic cloves	2
6 cups	Vegetable or chicken stock	1.5 litres
1/2 cup	White wine	125 ml
to taste	Salt and pepper	to taste
1/2 cup	Heavy cream (35%)	125 ml
1 bunch	Fresh basil, chopped	1 bunch

Preheat oven to 350° F (180° C).

Toss the vegetables and the garlic in the oil. Place on a sheet pan and roast for about 30 minutes until the vegetables are golden brown and soft. Now place in a soup pot, add the stock and wine and let simmer on a medium heat for about 1 hour. Purée the soup in the pot and add the salt and pepper to taste. Add the cream and let simmer until desired consistency is reached. Now add the chopped basil. You will want to wait to chop your herbs until just before you are ready to serve, so that they do not lose their flavour.

Ovenhead Smoked Salmon Crisps

2 oz.	Cream cheese	55 g
1 oz.	Ovenhead Smoked Salmon	30 g
1/2 tsp.	Cracked black pepper	2 ml
1 tsp.	Lemon zest	5 ml
1 tsp.	Dill	5 ml
1 sheet	Pre-rolled puff pastry, about 4-inches (10 cm) square	1 sheet

Combine cheese, smoked salmon, pepper, lemon zest and dill in a food processor and blend until smooth. Lay out puff pastry and spread on cheese mixture. Fold over the puff pastry in half and then cut into 3/4 inch (2 cm) strips. Twist the pastry to form a nice tight twist, bake at 350° F (180° C) until golden brown (approximately 10 minutes).

Serving suggestion: Serve warm on the side of the soup plate.

Roary MacPherson C.C.C., Executive Chef
The Fairmont Hotel Macdonald

Crispy Romaine and Endive Summer Salad
with Raspberry Maple Dill Dressing

Serves: 4

2 tbsp.	Pumpkin seeds	30 ml
1 tsp.	Olive oil	5 ml
pinch	Salt and pepper	pinch
1 head	Romaine lettuce, washed, dried and cut into 1 inch (25mm) pieces	1 head
2 heads	Belgian endive, core removed, cut julienne	2 heads
1	Fresh peach, pit removed, and thinly sliced	1
2	Oranges, peeled, seeded, and thinly sliced	2
5	Large strawberries, thinly sliced	5

Toss pumpkin seeds in olive oil and salt and pepper. Toast in a 350° F (180° C) oven for 10 minutes. Cut all ingredients and keep separate until service. When ready to serve, toss lettuce and fruit together in large bowl with raspberry dressing. Top with toasted pumpkin seeds.

Raspberry Maple Dill Dressing

1 cup	Plain yogurt	250 ml
1/2 cup	Olive oil	100 ml
1/2 cup	Raspberry vinegar	100 ml
1 tbsp.	Fresh dill, finely chopped	15 ml
2 tbsp.	Pure maple syrup	30 ml
to taste	Salt and pepper	to taste

Whisk all ingredients together in a bowl. Use with above salad.

Brian Leadbetter, Executive Chef
Madison's Grill — Union Bank Inn

Entrées

AAA Alberta Beef Tenderloin
topped with Tomato Basil Stew, Applewood Smoked Cheddar Toque, and Sweetgrass Jus

Serves: 1

Tomato and Basil Stew

1 cup	Water	250 ml
1/2 cup	Vinegar	125 ml
1/2 cup	Sugar	125 ml
3	Roma tomatoes, diced	3
1 bunch	Chiffonade of basil	1 bunch
to taste	Black pepper, cracked	to taste

Place water, vinegar and sugar in a pot and reduce until a syrup begins to form. Take off the heat and add the rest of the ingredients. Place back on the heat and cook for about 1 hour until the tomatoes are almost totally broken down.

Sweetgrass Jus

2 cups	Red wine	500 ml
1 tbsp.	Sweetgrass, trimmed, chopped (available in specialty shops like Debaji's)	15 ml

Add sweetgrass to wine and simmer for about 20 minutes. This will add the sweetgrass flavour to your sauce to give it that distinctive taste. Drain. Drizzle over the beef tenderloin, stew, and Applewood Smoked Cheddar toque.

AAA Alberta Beef Tenderloin

5 oz.	Beef tenderloin fillet	140 g
1 slice	Applewood Smoked Cheddar	1 slice

Cook tenderloin to your liking. Place a soup-spoon full of tomato basil stew on top and cover with the slice of cheese. Place in the preheated oven at 350° F (180° C) for about 45 seconds to melt the cheese. You do not want to melt the cheese too long.

Serving suggestion: Serve with starch and vegetable of your choice.

Roary MacPherson C.C.C., Executive Chef
The Fairmont Hotel Macdonald

Select Chicken Breast

Serves: 4

Mushroom Duxelle

2 tbsp.	Butter	30 ml
4 1/3 cups	White mushrooms, finely chopped	1 litre
4 oz.	Yellow onion, finely chopped	125 ml
2-3 oz.	White wine	60-75 ml
8 oz.	Whipping cream	250 ml

Sauté mushrooms and onion in butter. Add white wine and whipping cream. Simmer over low heat until wet ingredients are evaporated. Season with salt and pepper to taste.

Parmesan Batter

4	Eggs, beaten	4
8 oz.	Fresh Parmesan cheese, grated	250 ml

Blend egg and cheese until smooth.

Chicken

4 x 6 oz.	Chicken breasts, boneless, skinless	4 x 150 g
6 oz.	Mushroom duxelle (see above)	150 g
4 oz.	Smoked ham, thinly sliced	100 g
8 oz.	Parmesan batter (see above)	250 g
2 cups	All purpose flour	500 g

Preheat oven to 350° F (180° C).

Carefully slice breasts horizontally without cutting through back edge and open up like a book. Place equal portions of duxelle and ham on each breast and close breast together. Salt and pepper breasts, lightly dust with flour all over and coat evenly with Parmesan batter. Sauté in non-stick pan, turning when golden brown. Finish in oven for 7 to 10 minutes. Serve with your favourite vegetables or a salad.

Gordon Guiltner, Executive Chef
Café Select

Cumin-Chili Crusted Lamb Rack
with Grilled Potato and Eggplant Salad

Serves: 4

2	Whole lamb racks, frenched	2
1 tbsp.	Cumin, ground	15 ml
1 tbsp.	Fresh ground black pepper	15 ml
1 tsp.	Chili flakes	5 ml
1/2 tsp.	Cayenne (optional for extra zip)	2 ml
1 tsp.	Oregano, ground	5 ml
1 tsp.	Sea salt	5 ml
1 tsp.	Honey	5 ml
1 tsp.	Balsamic vinegar	5 ml

Blend all spices together. Mix honey and balsamic vinegar. Brush lamb with honey mixture and rub with spice mixture. Place on a baking pan. Cook in oven or on grill to desired temperature.

Balsamic Reduction

8 oz.	Balsamic vinegar	250 ml
8 oz.	Red wine, preferably Shiraz	250 ml
2 sprigs	Fresh rosemary	2 sprigs
1 oz.	Liquid honey	30 ml

Place all ingredients in a stainless steel pot (aluminum will not work), simmer over low heat until reduced by half. It should have a syrupy consistency. Let cool at room temperature until ready to use.

Cucumber Raita

1/2 cup	Yogurt	125 ml
1/2 cup	Sour cream	125 ml
1 oz.	Fresh dill, finely chopped	30 g
1/4 cup	Red onion, chopped	50 ml
1 tsp.	Fresh garlic, minced	5 ml
1/2	Long English cucumber, grated	1/2
2	Lemons, juiced	2
to taste	Salt and pepper	to taste

Mix all ingredients in a bowl and set aside in refrigerator.

Grilled Potato and Eggplant Salad

2	Yukon gold potatoes, cut into 1-inch (25mm) rounds	2
1/2	Red onion, cut into 2-inch (50 mm) rings	1/2
1	Eggplant, cut into 1-inch (25mm) rounds	1
1	Red pepper, cut into wedges	1
1 oz.	Olive oil	30 ml

Cook potatoes in simmering water for 8 minutes. Cool and pat dry. Brush all vegetables with oil and salt and pepper. Grill over high heat until soft and grill marked.

Assembly: Place vegetables on plate first. Slice lamb between bones and arrange on top. Drizzle balsamic reduction over meat and around plate. Top with cucumber raita.

Brian Leadbetter, Executive Chef
Madison's Grill — Union Bank Inn

Phyllo Chicken

Serves: 4

3	Chicken breasts, cooked, sliced and cooled	3
8	Phyllo pastry sheets (2 per serving)	8
2 oz.	Parmesan cheese	55 g
2 oz.	Feta cheese	55 g
2 oz.	Cheddar cheese	55 g
1 cup	Basil cream sauce (see below)	250 ml
	Butter, to brush on parcels	

Mix the three cheeses together. On a phyllo sheet, lay out one quarter of the chicken. Add 2 tbsp. (30 ml) of the cream sauce (see below) and top with the cheese mixture. Fold the sides of the phyllo sheet in first and then roll in the ends three times per side to seal. Double wrap with a second phyllo sheet. To cook, brush with butter and bake in the oven at 375° F (190° C) until both sides are golden brown, about 5 to 10 minutes. Remember to flip halfway through cooking.

Basil Cream Sauce

1 tbsp.	Garlic, chopped	15 ml
1 tbsp.	Basil paste	15 ml
1 cup	Chicken stock	250 ml
2 tbsp.	Cornstarch	30 ml
1/4 cup	Cold water	50 ml
1/3 cup	Heavy cream	75 ml

In a saucepan sauté the garlic and basil lightly. Add the chicken stock and bring to a boil. Blend the cornstarch with a little water. Add to pan to thicken sauce. Then add the cream. Mix well and set aside to cool.

Substitute: Salmon can be used instead of chicken if desired.

Chee Chu, Chef
Turtle Creek Café

Sautéed Beef Tenderloin
with Roasted Tomato and
Ancho Chili Sauce

Serves: 4-6

2 lbs.	Beef tenderloin, cut into 1/2-inch (12 mm) medallions	900 g
1/4 cup	Flour	50 ml
2 tbsp.	Cooking oil, to sear beef	30 ml

Roasted Tomato and Ancho Chili Sauce

8	Ripe tomatoes	8
2	Onions, quartered	2
4	Garlic cloves	4
2-3	Ancho chilies, dried	2-3
1/4 cup	Olive oil	50 ml
1 cup	Dry red wine	250 ml
1/2 tbsp.	Cumin	7 ml
2 1/2 cups	Beef stock, light	625 ml
to taste	Salt and pepper	to taste

Roast the tomatoes, onions and garlic for 20 to 30 minutes in a 400° F (200° C) oven. Reconstitute the chilies in boiling water for 10 minutes, strain, remove stems and purée with 1/4 cup (50 ml) olive oil. Reduce the wine by three-quarters, then add the chili purée, tomatoes, onions, garlic, cumin, and stock and simmer for 20 to 30 minutes. Season to taste.

Lightly toss beef in flour. Heat 2 tbsp. (30 ml) cooking oil in pan and sear beef. Reduce heat and cook to desired doneness. Top with sauce and serve.

Chuck Phillips, Owner/Chef
Highlevel Diner

Bison, Lamb and Black Bean Chili

Serves: 10

| 8 oz. | Black beans | 250 g |

Presoak the black beans in cold water overnight.

18 oz.	Bison stewing meat	500g
18 oz.	Lamb stewing meat	500g
1/4 cup	Olive oil	50 ml
4 oz.	Onions	125 g
2 oz.	Shallots	50 g
1/2 oz.	Garlic	15 g
1	Small green pepper, diced	1
1	Small red pepper, diced	1
1	Green onion, chopped	1
1/2	Jalapeno pepper, finely diced	1/2
14 oz.	Canned tomatoes, diced	450 g
14 oz.	Canned tomatoes, crushed	450 g
3 oz.	Tomato paste	85 g
1/2 oz.	Sugar	15 g
1 tsp.	Oregano, dried	5 ml
1 tsp.	Basil, dried	5 ml
1 tsp.	Thyme, dried	5 ml
1/2 cup	Molasses	100 ml
to taste	Salt and pepper	to taste

Sauté bison and lamb in olive oil until golden brown. Add vegetables and cook for 10 minutes. Add the canned tomato ingredients and continue to cook. Add the rest of the ingredients and cook for up to 8 hours or until meat is tender. Adjust seasoning. Let sit after cooking in the refrigerator overnight.

Serving suggestion: Reheat next day and serve with a corn and cheese biscuit.

Ross Munro, Executive Chef
Pradera Café and Lounge, The Westin

Savory Herb Roasted Chicken
with Cranberry Sage Jus

Serves: 4

4 x 8 oz.	Boneless chicken halves with skin on (wing bone in)	4 x 225 g
1	Bell pepper, roasted and julienned	1
4 pieces	Sundried peaches	4 pieces
4 tbsp.	Pine nuts, toasted	60 ml
6 oz.	Aged white cheddar cheese	160 g
to taste	Salt and pepper	to taste

Place chicken breasts skin side down between two pieces of plastic wrap. Pound chicken evenly away from bone and season. Discard plastic wrap. Place pepper, peaches, and pine nuts lengthwise across chicken and sprinkle cheese on top. Fold sides of chicken over, place skin side up on lightly oiled baking pan and bake at 375° F (190° C) for 20 to 25 minutes until golden brown.

Cranberry Sage Jus

1 pack	Fresh cranberries	1 pack
3 oz.	Dry red wine	85 ml
to taste	Sugar	to taste
1 tbsp.	Fresh sage, chopped	15 ml
to taste	Salt and pepper	to taste

Simmer cranberries in wine until soft. Add sugar and sage, blend until smooth. Strain and add salt and pepper.

Serving suggestion: Lorraine Ellis and Sabrina Warnholz, our wine stewards, recommend California's Stonehedge Merlot with this dish.

Cyrilles Koppert, Proprietor and Chris Davies, Chef
Manor Café

Seafood Pasta

Serves: 4

2 tbsp.	Olive oil	30 ml
1/2 cup	Onions, sliced	125 ml
1 tbsp.	Garlic, chopped	15 ml
1/3 lb.	Rock shrimp	150 g
1/3 lb.	Scallops	150 g
1 cup	Peppers, sliced	250 ml
4	Tomatoes, in wedges	4
1/4 cup	Olives	50 ml
1/2 tbsp.	Cajun spice	7 ml
to taste	Salt and pepper	to taste
1/4 cup	Fresh basil, chopped	50 ml
1/2 cup	Parmesan cheese	125 ml
	Pasta of your choice	

Heat pan with olive oil, sauté onion and garlic, then add seafood. Sauté until seafood is half cooked, add pepper, tomatoes, olives, and seasoning and continue cooking. Do not overcook the seafood. Mix cooked pasta with basil and cheese, then add the sautéed seafood, toss and serve.

Chee Chu, Chef
Turtle Creek Café

BBQ Oriental
Pork Tenderloin

Serves: 6

36-42 oz.	Pork tenderloins (3 or 4 whole)	1-1.2 kg
1 1/2 cups	Soya sauce	375 ml
1/2 cup	Water	125 ml
3 tbsp.	Fresh ginger, grated	45 ml
1 1/2 tbsp.	Fresh chopped herbs, such as rosemary, basil, or thyme	22 ml
2 tsp.	Garlic, crushed	10 ml
pinch	White pepper, cracked	pinch

Clean the pork tenderloin by removing the silver skin. Trim and cut into 6 to 8 oz. (170 to 225 g) portions. Mix soya sauce, water, ginger, herbs, garlic and pepper in a medium bowl. Marinate pork in refrigerator for 8 to 12 hours.

Preheat BBQ on a high heat. Sear the pork on all sides and lower the BBQ to medium low heat to finish cooking the pork (approximately 8 to 10 minutes). Remove the pork, slice into medallions and serve.

Paul Campbell, Executive Chef
Café de Ville

Beef Tataki

Serves: 3

8 oz.	Beef strip loin, well trimmed	225 g
4 oz.	White onion	115 g
2 tbsp.	Green onion, chopped	30 ml
1 tbsp.	Daikon, grated	15 ml

Cut white onion into very thin slices, wash and drain well. Place on a plate in one thin layer. Pan sear or grill steak lightly, just long enough so that outer meat changes colour. Immerse steak into bowl of ice-cold water for 5 seconds, then pat dry with a clean paper towel. Slice beef into very thin strips, then place slices on top of white onion layer. Sprinkle with chopped green onion and grated daikon, then add homemade Ponzu sauce. Hot pepper can be added if you prefer; it complements the flavours. Enjoy!

Ponzu Sauce

2 tbsp.	Sake	30 ml
7 tbsp.	Lemon juice, fresh	100 ml
7 tbsp.	Orange juice, fresh	100 ml
1/2 cup	Soy sauce	120 ml
1 piece	Dry kelp	1 piece

Heat sake in a saucepan then ignite the sake so that the alcohol is burned off. Be careful with this procedure as the flame could burn anything too close. Let alcohol-free sake cool off before adding lemon and orange juices, soy sauce and dry kelp. Let the mixture cool in the refrigerator for 2 hours.

Don Luong, Chef/Owner
EastBound Eatery

Spaghetti Trastaverini

Serves: 6

1 lb.	Spaghetti	450 g

Sauce

1/2 cup	Extra virgin olive oil	125 ml
1 1/2 tsp.	Salt	7 ml
4 tbsp.	Chopped fresh parsley	60 ml
2 tbsp.	Dried chili flakes	30 ml
1 cup	Chopped garlic	250 ml
1 lb.	Ground chicken	450 g
4 oz.	Black beans, precooked	125 g
3/4 cup	Tomato sauce	175 ml

In a large frying pan heat olive oil over medium heat. Add salt, parsley and chilies. Then add garlic and cook for 1 minute (being careful not to brown). Add chicken and cook, using a wooden spoon to break up chicken. Add cooked black beans and tomato sauce. Remove from heat, toss with cooked spaghetti and serve.

Kevin Lendrum, Executive Chef
Il Portico

Smoked Alberta Trout
with Yukon Gold Potato Risotto and Warm Beet Salad

Serves: 4

Potato Risotto

1 tbsp.	Olive oil	15 ml
1	Large shallot, finely minced	1
1 lb.	Yukon Gold potatoes, 1/8 inch (3mm) diced	450 g
3/4 cup	Chicken stock	175 ml
1/2 tsp.	Salt	2 ml
1/4 tsp.	Pepper	1 ml
2 oz.	Cheddar cheese, grated	55 g
2 oz.	Asiago cheese, grated	55 g

Place olive oil and shallots in a wide bottom pan over medium heat and cook shallots until soft. Add potatoes, stock, salt, and pepper and cook over low heat stirring constantly. The starch from the potatoes should release. Cook about 20 to 30 minutes. Stop when potatoes are 85% cooked — very firm but not crunchy. Add cheese and hold warm until service.

Beet Salad

3/4 lb.	Red beets, cooked, trimmed, 1/4 inch (5mm) dice	350 g
4 oz.	Red onion, 1/4 inch (5mm) dice	125 g
4 tbsp.	Balsamic vinegar	60 ml
1 tsp.	Black pepper	5 ml

Cook onions and vinegar over low heat until onions are very soft and syrupy. Season. Mix with beets and let stand 12 hours before serving.

Garnish

to taste	Walnut oil	to taste
to taste	Balsamic vinegar	to taste
8 oz.	Smoked trout	250 g

To serve, place about 4 tbsp. (60 ml) of warm risotto in centre of plate. Lightly place 3 small mounds of warm beet salad around perimeter of plate. Drizzle with walnut oil and a few drops of balsamic vinegar. Place smoked trout on top of potato risotto.

Substitute for trout: Any smoked fish of your choice.

Serving suggestion: The recommended wine with this dish is Fume Blanc or a Chardonnay

Larry Stewart C.C.C., Co-owner/Chef
Hardware Grill

Beef Wellington

Serves: 4

4 x 4 oz.	Beef tenderloin, cleaned	4 x 125 g
2 cups	Assorted mushrooms, such as shitake, portobello, oyster or button	500 ml
1/2	Onion	1/2
1	Garlic clove	1
to taste	Salt and pepper	to taste
1 sprig	Fresh rosemary	1 sprig
to taste	Characters Steak Spice	to taste
1	Egg	1
2	Puff pastry, sheets	2

Chop up mushrooms, onion and garlic. Add salt, pepper and rosemary; sauté in a little oil and set aside. Sear beef (don't forget to season it with "Characters Steak Spice" available at Characters). Whisk egg and with a pastry brush, brush onto the puff pastry sheets. Place beef on the puff pastry and put a big tablespoon of the mushroom mix on top. Wrap it up. Cut off the loose ends and pinch the sides together like a pie. Brush more egg on top and bake at 425° F (220° C) for about 20 minutes for medium rare.

Sauce

1	Shallot, chopped	1
1 tbsp.	Butter	15 ml
1 tbsp.	Flour	15 ml
2 cups	Beef stock	500 ml
1 cup	Raspberry vinegar	250 ml
1 cup	Sugar	250 ml
to taste	Salt and pepper	to taste

Sauté shallot in butter, then add flour to make a paste. Add beef stock, raspberry vinegar, sugar, salt, and pepper. Cook for about 20 minutes at a boil until sauce has the thickness of maple syrup.

Shonn Oborowsky, Executive Chef
Characters

Salt and Lemon Grilled Chicken
with Moroccan Olive Tapenade

Serves: 2

1	Chicken, medium size	1
to taste	Coarse salt	to taste
1 tbsp.	Olive oil	15 ml
1	Lemon, juiced	1

With backbone of chicken on a cutting board, cut through with a large chef's knife on each side of centre, thus removing backbone entirely. Turn chicken over and split cleanly in half along breastplate. Remove rib cage and thighbone if you wish. Season both halves of chicken with coarse salt, rub lightly with olive oil and grill on barbeque for approximately 20 minutes. Turn frequently and squeeze fresh lemon juice onto chicken after turning. Serve as is or with a piquant olive tapenade.

Moroccan Olive Tapenade

2 1/2 tsp.	Cumin seeds	10 ml
2 1/2 tsp.	Cardamom seeds	10 ml
2 1/2 tsp.	Coriander seeds	10 ml
1 1/2 tsp.	Cinnamon	7 ml
4 cups	Black olives, pitted	1 litre
to taste	Salt and cracked black pepper	to taste
	Water, as needed	

Toast seeds and cinnamon in skillet over high heat for 2 minutes. Grind finely in a spice grinder.

Purée olives in food processor, adding water to make a smooth paste. Season with spices, salt and pepper. Serve with the grilled chicken.

Donna Rumboldt, Chef/Owner
Donna at the Citadel

Bison Short Ribs

Serves: 4

3 lbs.	Bison short ribs 3/4" (1.5 cm) thick	1.5 kg
2 cups	Soy sauce	500 ml
3/4 cup	Pineapple juice	175 ml
1 cup	Sugar	250 ml
2 cups	Water	500 ml
1 tbsp.	Garlic, chopped	15 ml
1 tbsp.	Ginger root, freshly grated	15 ml

Brown ribs on both sides with a small amount of oil over medium-high heat. Transfer browned ribs to a shallow roasting pan. Combine the remaining ingredients in a medium saucepan and bring to a boil. Pour mixture over ribs, cover with foil and bake at 350° F (180° C) for 1 1/2 to 2 hours. When meat is fork tender, drain and discard fluid. Baste ribs liberally with barbecue sauce (see below) and bake an additional 10 to 15 minutes.

Black Coffee Barbecue Sauce

Yields: 7 cups (1.5 litres)

1 1/2 cups	Tomato based chili sauce	375 ml
1 cup	Hoisin sauce	250 ml
2 tbsp.	Ginger root, freshly grated	30 ml
1 cup	Sherry	250 ml
1 cup	Apple cider vinegar	250 ml
2 cups	Honey	500 ml
1 tbsp.	Thyme	15 ml
1 tbsp.	Pepper	15 ml
1 1/2 tbsp.	Salt	22 ml
1 cup	Espresso	250 ml

Combine all ingredients in a saucepan and bring to a boil. Reduce heat and simmer sauce gently for 10 to 15 minutes. Store unused sauce in the refrigerator.

Larry Stewart C.C.C., Co-owner/Chef
Hardware Grill

Honey Gingered Teriyaki Chicken

Serves: 4

4	Chicken breasts		4
to taste	Pepper		to taste
3 tbsp.	Liquid honey		45 ml
3 tbsp.	Soy sauce	.	40 ml
1 tsp.	Fresh ginger, grated		5 ml
pinch	Sesame seeds, roasted		pinch

Grill chicken breasts in a pan, on BBQ or roast in oven. Add a little pepper. Heat honey in a frying pan until it starts bubbling. Add cooked chicken breasts to the boiling honey and quickly add soy sauce and grated ginger. Turn the chicken over several times, so that the sauce coats each piece evenly. Do not over-cook as the sauce burns very easily. Sprinkle with some sesame seeds.

Serving suggestion: Serve with seasonal vegetable stir-fry and short grain rice.

Don Luong, Chef/Owner
EastBound Eatery

Hardware Grill's Bison Meatloaf
with Corn Cheddar Mash

Serves: 8-10

3/4 cup	Onion, 1/4 inch (5 mm) dice	175 ml
1/2 cup	Celery, 1/4 inch (5 mm) dice	125 ml
1/2 cup	Red pepper, 1/4 inch (5 mm) dice	125 ml
1 tbsp.	Cooking oil	15 ml
1 tbsp.	Salt	15 ml
1 tbsp.	Pepper	15 ml
1 1/2 tbsp.	Thyme	22 ml
1 tbsp	Garlic, crushed	15 ml
2 tsp.	Juniper berries, ground	10 ml
1 1/2 lbs.	Ground bison	700 g
1 1/2 lbs.	Ground veal	700 g
3	Eggs	3
12	Bacon slices	12

Sauté onion, celery and red pepper in a small amount of oil until the onions are soft and translucent. Add the salt, pepper, thyme, garlic and ground juniper. Cool and drain. Mix all of the ingredients, including ground bison, ground veal and eggs, until well mixed preferably in an electric mixer with a paddle. Line a 5 x 10 inch (12 x 25 cm) bread pan with approximately 12 bacon slices. Fill bread pan to the top with the mixture and lay 5 strips of bacon across the top. Cover tightly with foil. Bake at 350° F (180° C) for 1 hour and 20 minutes, making sure the internal temperature is 155° F (70° C). Let stand for 20 minutes before slicing, or cool completely. Slice into 3/4-inch (2 cm) slices and reheat gently in microwave when ready to serve.

Serving suggestion: Serve with McNally's Ale onion sauce and corn Cheddar mash. Zinfandel or Shiraz wines complement this dish.

McNally's Ale Onion Sauce

1 cup	Onion, 1/4 inch (5 mm) diced	250 ml
1 oz.	Butter	30 g
1 bottle	McNally's Ale	1 bottle
2 cups	Demi glaze	500 ml

Caramelize the onion in the butter until dark and syrupy. Add the McNally's Ale and the demi glaze to the onion. Bring to a simmer and then cool.

Corn Cheddar Mashed Potatoes

Serves: 4-6

4	Red or white new potatoes, unpeeled and quartered	4
1/3 cup	Butter, melted	75 ml
1/3 cup	Sour cream	75 ml
1/2 tsp.	Salt	2 ml
1/2 tsp.	Pepper	2 ml
1/4 cup	Milk or cream	50 ml
8 oz.	Cheddar cheese, grated	250 g
8 oz.	Roasted corn	250 g
1/4 cup	Parsley, chopped	50 ml

Boil potatoes until fully cooked, drain well. Mash potatoes with skin on, add butter, sour cream, salt, pepper and cream. Potatoes should be a little bit chunky. Fold in the Cheddar, corn and parsley. Keep warm in oven until ready to serve.

Larry Stewart C.C.C., Co-owner/Chef
Hardware Grill

Salmon in Roasted Tomato Broth
with Potato and Fennel and Fresh Herb Salad

Serves: 4

Tomato Broth

20	Ripe Roma tomatoes	20

Roast tomatoes at 350° F (180° C) until very soft and slightly browned. Extract juice from tomatoes while still hot by pushing through a fine mesh sieve with a ladle. Discard solids and strain liquid through the sieve again until broth is clear. Set aside and reheat for service.

Salmon

4 x 6 oz.	Salmon fillets	4 x 170 g

Salmon can be grilled, poached, baked, sautéed or cooked using your favourite method until desired doneness.

Herb Salad

Equal parts with leaves picked and stems removed:

	Basil	
	Mint	
	Chives	
	Flat leaf parsley	
	Tarragon	
	Chervil	
	Salad leaves	
1/2	Lemon, juice	1/2
2 tbsp.	Extra virgin olive oil	30 ml
to taste	Salt and pepper	to taste

Potato and Fennel Accompaniment

2 oz.	Pancetta, diced	120 g
2 oz.	Extra virgin olive oil	60 ml
1	Medium onion, diced	1
6	Garlic cloves, chopped	6
16	Baby potatoes, quartered and par-boiled	16
1	Fennel bulb, cored and shaved	1
1	Lemon, juice	1
10 sprigs	Flat leaf parsley	10 sprigs
to taste	Sea salt and fresh black pepper	to taste
8	Sun dried tomatoes, reconstituted and julienned for garnish	8

In a large skillet over medium high heat, sauté pancetta in olive oil until brown but still soft. Add onion, garlic and par-boiled potatoes; cook until onions are soft and potatoes are heated through. Add shaved fennel and cook for about two minutes. Finish with lemon juice, parsley and salt and pepper.

Assembly: Divide vegetables into four serving bowls. Ladle in some of the tomato broth. Place cooked fish on the vegetables. Top fish with some of the herb salad and garnish with sun dried tomatoes.

Kevin Lendrum, Executive Chef
Il Portico

Machhli Kebab
(Marinated Salmon)

Serves: 2

1 lb	Fresh Atlantic salmon cut into 2-inch (5 cm) squares	500 g

Marinade

1 cup	Yogurt	250 ml
1 tbsp.	Canola oil	15 ml
1 tbsp.	Lemon juice	15 ml
pinch	Orange/red colour	pinch
1 tbsp.	Fresh garlic paste	15 ml
1/2 tbsp.	Fresh ginger paste	8 ml
1 tsp.	Ground cumin	5 ml
2 tsp.	Garam masala	10 ml
1 tsp.	Kastoori methi	5 ml
1 tsp.	Carom seed	5 ml
1 tsp.	Salt	5 ml
1 tsp.	Chaat masala	5 ml

Mix all ingredients except chaat masala. Marinate the cubes of salmon in the refrigerator for two hours. Preheat oven to 350° F (180° C). Place the marinated salmon on an oven tray and bake in the oven for 30 to 40 minutes.

Serving suggestion: Put on a plate and sprinkle with chaat masala and garnish with lemon and cucumber slices. Serve with hot rice or bread.

Spices

Garam masala is mixture of spices containing black pepper, cardamom, cinnamon, cloves and cumin. See recipe for chaat masala opposite. These spice blends can be purchased at Indian markets. Kasoori methi is dried fenugreek leaves — celery leaves can be used instead. Carom seeds, or Bishop's weed, look like small caraway seeds and taste like a pungent version of thyme. Dried thyme, cumin or caraway can be substituted for carom seeds.

Chaat Masala

1 tbsp.	Dried mango powder	15 ml
1 tsp.	Cumin	5 ml
1 tsp.	Ground black salt	5 ml
1 tsp.	Ground coriander	5 ml
3/4 tsp.	Ground ginger	3 ml
1/2 tsp.	Salt	2 ml
1/2 tsp.	Ground pepper	2 ml
1/2 tsp.	Red pepper	2 ml

Heat a skillet and dry roast spices together until aromatic.

Victor D'Alves, Director
Khazana Restaurant

Smoked Pancetta, Buffalo Mozzarella, and Savoy Cabbage Risotto

Serves: 6

4 oz.	Smoked pancetta	125 g
1	Garlic clove, sliced	1
1/2 head	Savoy cabbage, thinly sliced	1/2 head
to taste	Salt and ground pepper	to taste
1	Red onion, medium	1
1/2 cup	Butter, unsalted	125 ml
2 cups	Arborio rice	500 ml
2/3 cup	White wine, dry	150 ml
6 cups	Chicken stock, heated	1.5 litres
2	Buffalo mozzarella balls, cut into small pieces	2
1 1/4 cup	Fresh parmesan cheese, grated	300 ml

Slice pancetta into matchsticks. Fry with garlic until golden brown. Toss in the cabbage. Place a lid on the pan and steam for about 5 minutes. Season with salt and pepper. Remove from the heat and set aside. Chop red onion very finely. Heat a heavy-bottomed saucepan and melt butter. When the butter starts to foam, add the onion and cook over low heat until soft, but not brown; about 2 to 3 minutes. Add the rice and stir continuously for about 3 minutes or until the rice becomes opaque. Pour in the white wine and allow to absorb. Start adding simmering stock to the rice, ladle by ladle, stirring all the time. The rice is cooked when it has a thick, creamy consistency and an even, al dente bite to the grain. Incorporate the cooked pancetta and the savoy cabbage mixture. Fold in the cheeses. Season and serve.

Patrizio Sacchetto, Master Chef
Via Vai

Shrimp Piquante

Serves: 2

1 tbsp.	Cooking oil	15 ml
3	Fresh garlic cloves, thinly sliced	3
1	Red pepper, diced	1
1	Green pepper, diced	1
1/2 cup	White onion, diced	125 ml
1/4 cup	Green onion, diced	50 ml
16	Large shrimp, peeled and de-veined	16
1/2 cup	Chicken stock	125 ml
1/4 cup	Fresh parsley, finely chopped	50 ml
1/4 cup	Frank's Red Hot Sauce	50 ml

Heat oil and sauté garlic, peppers, onions and shrimp. Deglaze with stock. Add hot sauce and reduce. Just before serving add parsley and toss.

Serving suggestion: Serve with rice or linguine.

Russ Paranich, Sous Chef
Louisiana Purchase Restaurant

Ostrich Steak
with Cassis and Saskatoon Berries

Serves: 2

4 x 3 oz.	Ostrich steaks	4 x 85 g
1 oz.	Red wine	30 ml
2 tbsp.	Cassis or blackcurrant syrup	30 ml
1/4 cup	Saskatoon berries	50 ml
1 tbsp.	Fresh garlic, minced	15 ml
1 tbsp.	Shallots	15 ml
to taste	Salt and pepper	to taste
1/2 cup	Demi glaze (or brown sauce)	125 ml

In a preheated frying pan at medium high, sear the ostrich and then remove from pan. Deglaze with red wine. Add cassis, saskatoon berries, garlic, shallots, salt and pepper to taste. Add demi glaze to pan and turn down heat to medium. Reduce sauce to desired consistency, return ostrich to pan and finish cooking to desired temperature.

Serving suggestion: Serve with your favourite fresh vegetables and starch.

Cui Kouch, Chef de cuisine
Normand's

Hazelnut Encrusted Rack of Lamb
with Rosemary and Balsamico Sauce

Serves: 4

1 cup	Hazelnuts, shelled, skins removed	250 ml

In a hot oven, roast hazelnuts until golden brown. Let them cool, and then grind them to almost a powder in a blender. Reserve.

Rosemary and Balsamico Sauce

1	Onion, diced	1
1 cup	Balsamic vinegar	250 ml
4 cups	Stock, lamb, veal or bouillon	1 litre
1 tsp.	Rosemary	5 ml

Sweat the onion in a pot for 4 minutes. Add rosemary and vinegar. Season to your liking. Reduce by two-thirds. Add stock and reduce again by two-thirds. Strain through a fine sieve.

Lamb

4	Rack of lamb, frenched	4
1 tbsp.	Oil	15 ml
1 tsp.	Dijon mustard	5 ml

Preheat the oven to 375° F (180° C)

Heat the oil in a frying pan and put the racks of lamb, meat part down, in the pan. Let them brown for 2 minutes and finish cooking in the oven: 15 minutes for medium rare or when the internal temperature of the meat reaches 165 ° F (75° C). Remove the lamb from the oven. Let it cool down a bit, then brush with the mustard. Coat the lamb with the ground hazelnuts.

Serving suggestion: Cut the racks in the middle along the bones, then lean them over a bed of vegetables of your liking. Pour the sauce around the plate.

Eric Plantier, Executive Chef
Plantier's

Black Bean Chili

Serves: 8-10

1 lb.	Black beans	450 g
2	Bay leaves	2
1 tsp.	Chilies, crushed	5 ml

Soak beans for 24 hours. Rinse several times. Cover with water, add bay leaves and crushed chilies and simmer for 2 hours or until tender. Drain, rinse and set aside.

2	Chipotle peppers	2
1	Ancho peppers	1
2	Passillas peppers	2
4	Garlic cloves	4
1 tbsp.	Oregano	15 ml
2 1/2 tbsp.	Cumin	40 ml
1/2 tbsp.	Black pepper	7 ml
1 tbsp.	Salt	15 ml
1/2–3/4 cup	Olive oil	125–175 ml
1 1/2 cups	Onion, diced	375 ml
40 oz.	Plum tomatoes, drained and crushed	1.2 kg

Reconstitute dried peppers in water and simmer, covered, for 30 minutes. Seed peppers and purée with garlic, oregano, cumin, salt and pepper, and olive oil.

Sauté onions with paste on medium heat. Add beans and tomatoes and simmer uncovered for 1 hour. Adjust seasoning and serve.

Chuck Phillips, Owner/Chef
Highlevel Diner

Paddle River Organic Rabbit
with Smoked Wild Boar Bacon Ragout and Sweet Potato Pie

Serves: 4

Sweet Potato Pie

2 cups	Yams, cooked, mashed	500 ml
1	Onion, minced, sautéed	1
1 tbsp.	Brown sugar	15 ml
2 tsp. each	Sherry and brandy	10 ml each
1 tsp. each	Cinnamon and ground ginger	5 ml each
1/8 tsp. each	Allspice and nutmeg	0.5 ml each
1 tbsp. each	Lemon juice and zest	15 ml each
1/4 cup	Pecans, chopped	50 ml
1/2 cup	Orange juice	125 ml
2	Eggs, separated	2

Preheat oven to 350° F (180° C). Mix all ingredients into mashed yams including egg yolks. Whip egg whites and fold into yam mixture at the end. Bake for 40 to 50 minutes.

Rabbit

2 tbsp.	Olive oil	30 ml
2 oz.	Smoked boar bacon, diced	55 g
1/4 cup	Onion, diced	50 ml
1 lb.	Rabbit, 1/2-inch cubes	500 g
1 oz.	Shitake mushrooms, sliced	30 g
1 oz.	Portabello mushrooms, sliced	30 g
1 oz.	White button mushrooms, sliced	30 g
3/4 cup	Veal jus or heavy beef stock	175 ml
1 tsp.	Tarragon	5 ml
1/4 cup	Heavy cream	50 ml

Heat olive oil. Fry bacon until partially rendered. Add onions and sauté until transparent. Add rabbit and sauté until cooked. Add mushrooms and sauté. Add veal jus or stock and tarragon, simmer for 10 minutes. Add cream, salt and pepper to taste. Regular bacon may be substituted for boar bacon. Serve with a slice of potato pie.

Jasmin Kobajica, Executive Chef
La Ronde, Chateau Lacombe

Halibut in Roasted Red and Green Pepper Sauces

Serves: 4

Roasted Red Pepper Sauce

2	Red bell peppers	2
2 tbsp.	Olive oil	30 ml
1/4 cup	Onions, coarsely chopped	50 ml
1 tsp.	Fresh garlic, minced	5 ml
1 tbsp.	Fresh basil, chopped	15 ml
to taste	Salt and pepper	to taste
1 1/4 cups	Chicken stock	300 ml

Place peppers in a 425° F (220° C) oven and roast. Turn peppers several times until the skin is charred; about 15 minutes. When skin is dark and blistered, remove from oven and place in a container, cover and cool in the refrigerator. When cool, peel off the skins with your fingers and chop coarsely. Combine the roasted peppers with oil, onion, garlic, basil, salt and pepper in a medium saucepan over high heat. Cook for 3 minutes, then stir in chicken stock and bring to a boil. Remove from heat and purée in a blender.

Roasted Green Pepper Sauce

Follow recipe for roasted red pepper sauce except substitute green peppers for red and 1 tsp. (5 ml) fresh dill in place of the basil.

Halibut

4 x 5 oz.	Halibut fillets	4 x 140 g
to taste	Salt and pepper	to taste
1/2 cup	Black sesame seeds	125 ml
1/4 cup	Canola oil	50 ml
	Lime slices for garnish	

Season fillets with salt and pepper and dredge in black sesame seeds. Heat oil in large cast iron frying pan, place fillets in pan and cook 5 to 6 minutes per side or until cooked all the way through.

Assembly: Place on warmed serving plates. Pour pepper sauces over the fish in a decorative way. Garnish with lime wedges.

Dennis Vermette, Executive Chef
Louisiana Purchase Restaurant

Seven Spices Roasted Salmon
with Tomato and Star Anise Sauce

Serves: 4

2 lbs.	Salmon fillet	1 kg
1 tsp.	Allspice	5 ml
1 tsp.	Curry powder	5 ml
1 tsp.	Coriander powder	5 ml
1 tsp.	Ginger, ground	5 ml
pinch	Cardamom	pinch
pinch	Star anise powder	pinch
small pinch	Clove powder	small pinch

Divide the salmon fillet into four portions. Blend all the spices together and dust the fillets with the spice mixture on all sides. Set aside and marinate in the refridgerator for 2 to 4 hours.

Preparing Salmon

1 tsp.	Olive oil	5 ml

Preheat oven to 375° F (180° C).

Pour olive oil into a non-stick, ovenproof pan. Heat on the stove. When the oil is fairly hot, place salmon in the pan flesh side down and let it colour slightly. Finish by baking in the oven for approximately 8 minutes.

Tomato and Star Anise Sauce

1	Onion	1
1 tbsp.	Butter	15 ml
6 cups	Fish stock	1.5 litres
5 1/2 oz.	Tomato paste	156 ml
1	Orange, juiced, reserve peel	1
2	Star anise	2
to taste	Salt, pepper, cayenne pepper	to taste
to taste	Cream (optional)	to taste
pinch	Cayenne	pinch

Dice the onion and cook in the butter until soft. Add fish stock, tomato paste, orange peel and orange juice, plus the star anise. Season with salt, pepper and a pinch of cayenne. Cook until sauce has reduced to about two-thirds. Pass the sauce through a fine sieve. At this point, you can add some cream to round it up but this is optional.

Serving suggestion: Place the salmon on a bed of cooked vegetables of your liking, and pour the sauce around it. At the restaurant, we serve this dish with some spinach quickly sautéed in olive oil and garlic along with deep fried leeks.

Eric Plantier, Executive Chef
Plantier's

Pyrogies

Yields: 20 pyrogies

Pyrogy Dough

2	Eggs	2
1 cup	Warm water	250 ml
2 tbsp.	Vegetable oil	30 ml
4 cups	Flour	1 litre
2 tbsp.	Salt	30 ml

Beat the eggs and add to the water and vegetable oil. Blend well, then add flour and salt. Knead dough until smooth and soft. Cover dough and let rest for 30 minutes. Roll out thin. Cut into squares or rounds. Place a teaspoon of filling (see below) on each piece, pinch edges together well to seal. Drop into boiling salted water and boil for about 8 minutes. Strain in a colander and pour 1 cup (250 ml) cold water over them. Drain, place in dish, sprinkle with oil. Toss gently to coat evenly.

Filling for Pyrogies

To make a basic, potato-based pyrogy filling, start with:

2 cups	Mashed potato	500 ml

Mix thoroughly with:

1/2 cup	Dry cottage cheese	125 ml
1/2 cup	**or** onion, chopped, sautéed	125 ml
1/2 cup	**or** aged Cheddar cheese	125 ml
to taste	Salt and pepper	to taste

Mushroom and Sour Cream Sauce

Yields: 2 cups

3 tbsp.	Butter	45 ml
2 tbsp.	Onion, minced	30 ml
1	Garlic clove, minced	1
2 tbsp.	Flour	30 ml
1 cup	Sour cream	250 ml
1 lb.	Mushrooms	450 g
to taste	Salt and pepper	to taste

Cook onion and garlic in butter until soft, do not brown. Add mushrooms and 1/2 cup (125 ml) of sour cream. Simmer for 5 minutes. Blend the flour with the other 1/2 cup (125 ml) cream and add to the mushroom mixture. Simmer for 20 minutes longer. If canned mushrooms are used, use two cans and add extra flour to thicken.

Serving suggestion: Serve with fried onions and/or mushroom and sour cream sauce, and vegetables of your choice.

Marge Choma, Chef/Owner
The Pyrogy House, The Pyrogy House Cook Book

Edgeland Ranch Bison Burger
with Red Onion Marmalade

Serves: 4

1 lb.	Ground bison	500 g
1/4 tsp.	Ground black pepper	1 ml
1 tsp.	Worcestershire sauce	5 ml
4 tsp.	Tomato paste or ketchup	20 ml
1 tsp.	Dijon mustard	5 ml
2 tsp.	Horseradish	10 ml

Mix all ingredients in a bowl and make into patties. Bison is very lean so grill slowly over low heat to keep in juices.

Red Onion Marmalade

Yields: 3 cups (750 ml)

1 lb.	Red onions, sliced thin	500 g
1	Orange, zest	1
1/3 cup	Red wine vinegar	75 ml
1/3 cup	Raspberry vinegar	75 ml
2/3 cup	White sugar	150 ml
1	Jalapeno, diced	1
1/2 tsp.	**or** crushed chilli	2 ml

Simmer over low heat until all ingredients are cooked and until nearly dry. Chill. You can store this in the fridge for 4 to 5 days or freeze it.

Serving suggestion: Place burger on a sour-dough bun, add a slice of aged Cheddar and top with a heaping spoonful of red onion marmalade.

Jasmin Kobajica, Executive Chef
La Ronde, Châteaux Lacombe

Lemongrass Chicken

Serves: 2

1 tbsp.	Cooking oil	15 ml
1 cup	Chicken, skinned, sliced	250 ml
1	Fresh garlic clove, minced	1
1 tsp.	Lemongrass, finely chopped	5 ml
1 tsp.	Dried chilli peppers	5 ml
2 tsp.	Fish sauce	10 ml
2 tsp.	Water	10 ml
1 tsp.	Sugar	5 ml
1/4 cup	Chicken broth	50 ml
1 tsp.	Potato starch or cornstarch	5 ml

Heat oil in a wok or a large bottomed pan. Add chicken and stir. Immediately add garlic, lemongrass and chilli pepper. Cook for 1 minute. Mix fish sauce with water and sugar and then add to wok. Add chicken broth and continue to stir fry for 5 minutes. Add the starch mixed with cold water until the sauce begins to thicken.

Serving suggestion: Serve over steamed rice or rice noodles and your favourite vegetables.

Tanya, Chef
Lemongrass Café

Pan-Seared Lemongrass Ostrich
with Hot and Sour Beet Jus and
Lotus Leaf-Steamed Risotto

Serves: 6

Pan-Seared Ostrich

6 x 6 oz.	Ostrich tenderloins	6 x 170 g
2	Lemongrass stalks, finely chopped	2
1 1/2 tbsp.	Fresh ginger, minced	23 ml
4	Garlic cloves, minced	4
2 tbsp.	Hot bean sauce	30 ml
2 tbsp.	Soy sauce	30 ml
3 tbsp.	Dry Marsala wine	45 ml
2 tsp.	Fresh lime juice	10 ml
1 tbsp.	Sugar	15 ml
1 tsp.	Salt	5 ml

Mix all of the above ingredients in a large bowl and marinate the ostrich for at least 4 hours or overnight. Preheat the oven to 400° F (200° C). Pan sear the ostrich on both sides on high heat and then cook in the oven until medium rare, about 8 to 10 minutes, depending on thickness.

Hot and Sour Beet Jus

Yields: 1 cup (250 ml), serves 6-8

1 tbsp.	Cooking oil	15 ml
2	Medium shallots, chopped	2
1/4 cup	Aged Chinese vinegar	50 ml
	or red wine vinegar	
1/4 cup.	Brown sugar	50 ml
1/2 cup	Red wine	125 ml
1 lb.	Beets, peeled and sliced	500 g
1 tsp.	Chili sauce	5 ml
2 cups	Chicken stock	500 ml
to taste	Salt and pepper	to taste

Heat cooking oil in a saucepan and sauté the shallots until light brown. Add vinegar and brown sugar. Reduce the liquid to one third. Add the red wine and reduce by half. Add beets, chili sauce and chicken stock. Simmer for about 30 minutes on low heat and reduce. Season with salt and pepper to taste. Strain the liquid through a sieve. The sauce can be thickened with cornstarch, blended with a little cold water, if desired. The jus can be made ahead and refrigerated for up to 4 days.

(Continued on following page)

Lotus Leaf-Steamed Risotto
(continued)

Serves: 3 or 6

1	Turkey breast	1
2 tbsp.	Olive oil	30 ml
3	Shallots, sliced	3
1 1/2 cups	Arborio rice	375 ml
1/2 cup	White wine	125 ml
3 cups	Chicken stock	750 ml
1 tbsp.	Olive oil	15 ml
1/2 cup	Roasted corn	125 ml
1/2 cup	Green peas	125 ml
3-4	Shitake mushrooms	3-4
1/4 cup	Sweet red pepper	50 ml
1/4 cup	Parmesan cheese, grated	50 ml
1/4 cup	Mozzarella cheese, grated	50 ml
3	Dry lotus leaves	3
1 tbsp.	Olive oil	15 ml
2	Scallions, finely chopped	2
2	Garlic cloves, minced	2

Grill the turkey breast for 10 minutes or until 80% cooked and cut it into small pieces. Set aside. Heat the chicken stock. Heat the olive oil in a stock pot and sauté the shallots. Add the rice and white wine. Add the heated chicken stock to the rice mixture 1/2 cup (125 ml) at a time and keep stirring the rice until half cooked. Transfer the rice mixture to a tray to cool. Sauté the roasted corn, peas, mushrooms, and red pepper in a frying pan and transfer to the rice. Let it cool and add cheeses. Add chopped, grilled turkey. Salt and pepper to taste. Risotto can be prepared 1 day before.

Soak the lotus leaves in hot water for 2 minutes and towel dry. Brush a little olive oil on the inside of the leaves, spoon the rice mixture onto each leaf and wrap it up, the same way you would wrap up a burrito. Steam for 10 minutes. If you have prepared the risotto and wrapped it in the lotus leaves ahead of time, wrap them in plastic wrap and store in the refrigerator. Bring to room temperature and steam for about 20 minutes or heat them in the microwave.

Assembly: Place ostrich on a plate and drizzle jus around it. Slice open the lotus leaf risotto for one serving or divide in two for two servings.

Serving suggestions: Serve with a Shiraz or a new world Merlot.

Judy Wu, Executive Chef
Polos Café

Bouillabaisse
(Seafood stew)

Serves: 6

Preparing Bouillabaisse for 6 servings

1	Carrot, small	1
3	Celery stalks	3
1	Red onion, small	1
1	Red pepper	1
1	Leek	1
1	Garlic clove, minced	1
pinch each	Basil and oregano	pinch each
1 tbsp.	Olive oil	15 ml
5	Fresh tomatoes, seeded, chopped	5
6 cups	Fish stock	1.5 litres
pinch	Saffron	pinch
3 tbsp.	Tomato paste	45 ml

Chop carrots, celery, red onion, red pepper and leek into 1/4-inch (5 cm) pieces. Sauté with minced garlic, basil and oregano. Add tomatoes, fish stock, saffron and tomato paste. Bring to a boil and reduce heat to simmer. Simmer for 40 to 45 minutes. The bouillabaisse can be made in advance to this stage and stored in refrigerator for several days. Bring bouillabaisse back to boiling when you are ready to cook the seafood and serve.

Seafood suggestions for Bouillabaisse
per person — adjust amounts according to servings

3	Prawns	3
3	Scallops	3
2 oz.	Fresh fish, such as salmon, halibut or cod	55 grams
4-5	Mussels	4-5
2 oz.	Calamari	55 grams
1	Crab claw	1
1	Garlic clove, minced	1
2	Shallots	2
to taste	Salt and pepper	to taste
1/4 cup	White wine	50 ml
1	Potato, diced and boiled	1

Preparing Seafood

If you are going to serve the bouillabaisse family style, the seafood can be cooked all together in one large pan and served in one large serving bowl. For a more formal, classic service, prepare seafood servings individually and serve in warmed soup bowls.

For each serving sauté seafood in a deep-sided pan with butter or oil, minced garlic, shallots, salt and pepper. Deglaze with white wine. Remove seafood from the pan and add 10 to 12 oz. (375 ml) of Bouillabaisse to pan. Bring to a boil. At this point you add the boiled potatoes to the dish or alternately serve with rice on the side. Return seafood to pan and simmer another 2 to 3 minutes or until fish is cooked, but not over done.

Serving suggestions: Serve with bread.

Jason Munn, Chef de cuisine
The Copper Pot Restaurant

Linguini Jambalaya

Serves: 4

8 oz.	Linguini	250 g
3 tbsp.	Butter	45 ml
2 x 8 oz.	Chicken breasts, sliced	2 x 250 g
1	Onion, large, finely chopped	1
24	Tiger prawns, shelled	24
6 oz.	Crab meat	170 g
1	Red pepper, large, julienned	1
1	Green pepper, large, julienned	1
2 cups	Mushrooms, sliced	500 ml
1 1/2 cups	Heavy cream	375 ml
4-6 tbsp.	Frank's Red Hot Sauce	50-80 ml
1/4 cup	Parmesan cheese	50 ml

Bring water to a boil in a large saucepan and add salt. Add pasta and cook until al dente. Strain. Melt butter in a large saucepan. Sauté sliced chicken and onion in butter until just under cooked. Add prawns and crab meat. When prawns are about half cooked, add peppers, mushrooms, and heavy cream. Simmer over a medium heat until mixture thickens to a sauce-like consistency, about 10 minutes. Add hot sauce and parmesan cheese and toss.

Serving suggestion: Serve with a tossed salad and a glass of white wine.

Carole DeAngelis
Carole's Café and Frank's Place

Desserts

White Chocolate Crème Brûlée

Serves: 4

3	Eggs	3
2	Egg yolks	2
1/3 cup	Sugar	75 ml
2 cups	Real whipping cream	500 ml
3/4 cup	White chocolate, melted	175 ml
1/4 cup	White Crème de Cacao liqueur	60 ml
	Superfine sugar to caramelize	
	Fresh fruit and cookies for garnish	

Combine eggs, yolks and sugar in a bowl and whisk until smooth. Heat the whipping cream until scalded, or just below the boiling point — do not boil. Add the melted chocolate and Crème de Cacao to the cream, blend, then slowly add to the egg mixture. Whisk until combined. Strain through a fine sieve, then pour into four 6 oz. (170 g) ceramic baking dishes. Bake at 300° F (150° C) in a water bath for approximately 1 hour, until the custards are set around the edges. The area in the middle should not be completely firm. Refrigerate for several hours or overnight. To serve, sprinkle each custard with 1 1/2 tbsp. (22 ml) of sugar and place 2 inches (5cm) under a preheated broiler until the sugar is melted and dark brown. Allow sugar to harden before serving. Garnish with fresh fruit and your favourite cookie.

Tip: Put the custards in a pan of ice water when under the broiler to keep them firm while the sugar is caramelizing.

Larry Stewart C.C.C., Co-owner/Chef
Hardware Grill

Pumpkin, Spiced Rum and Cream Cheese Soufflé

Serves: 2

4 tbsp.	Cream cheese	60 ml
4 tbsp.	Pumpkin purée	60 ml
2 tbsp.	Brown sugar	30 ml
1/2 oz.	Rum	15 g
pinch	Cinnamon	pinch
4	Eggs, separated	4
3 tbsp.	Granulated sugar	45 ml

Cream together cream cheese, pumpkin, brown sugar, rum and cinnamon. Separate the eggs into two bowls. Whisk whites with granulated sugar until medium peaks form. Add cream cheese mixture to the egg yolks. Fold the two mixtures together. Butter and sugar a ramekin, fill with mixture up to 1/2 inch (15 mm) below top. Bake at 425° F (220° C) until soufflé has risen 1 inch (25 mm) above the ramekin. Serve immediately with pumpkin caramel sauce.

Pumpkin Caramel Sauce

1 cup	Butter	250 ml
2 cups	Brown sugar	500 ml
1/4 cup	Corn syrup	50 ml
1/2 cup	Pumpkin purée	125 ml
1/2 tsp.	Cinnamon	2 ml
1/2 tsp.	Nutmeg	2 ml
1 cup	Cream	250 ml

Combine all ingredients in a heavy saucepan. Cook over medium heat until sugar is no longer grainy. Allow to cool slightly.

Shonn Oborowsky, Executive Chef
Characters

Panna Cotta with Figs, Port, Honey, and Lavender

Serves: 4

2 1/2	Gelatin leaves	2 1/2
1 1/2 cups	Buttermilk	350 ml
4 oz.	Crème fraîche (sour cream)	120 g
1 cup	Whipping cream	270 ml
4 oz.	Sugar	120 g
1	Vanilla bean, split	1

Soak gelatin leaves in luke warm water until soft. In a bowl mix together buttermilk and crème fraîche. Bring cream, sugar and vanilla to a boil in a saucepan. Reduce heat and simmer for 5 minutes. Remove from heat, take out vanilla bean and stir in gelatin. Temper the cream by adding 1/3 of the buttermilk mixture. Stir and add remainder of buttermilk. Strain mixture through a fine mesh sieve. Scrape the seeds of the vanilla bean into the mixture. Stir and divide liquid into four 4 oz. (125 g) ramekins. Let set in refrigerator for at least 3 hours. To serve, run a knife around the inside of the ramekin. Invert onto a plate and spoon sauce around the panna cotta.

Fig, Port, and Lavender Sauce

2 cups	Ruby port	500 ml
1/2 tbsp.	Dried lavender	7 ml
1 tbsp.	**or** fresh lavender	15 ml
12	Dried black mission figs, stemmed and cut in half	12
1 cup	Honey	250 ml

In a saucepan bring port and lavender to a boil and reduce by half. Strain out lavender. Add figs and honey to port and reduce to a syrupy consistency. Cool and set aside until service.

Kevin Lendrum, Executive Chef
Il Portico

Blueberry Crisp

Serves: 12

8 cups	Blueberries	2 litres
1	Lemon, zest	1
2/3 cup	White sugar	150 ml
1/4 cup	Cornstarch	50 ml

Mix all ingredients together and pour into a 9 x 13 inch (22 x 32 cm) baking pan. Add crisp topping (see below) and bake at 300° F (150° C) for 20 to 30 minutes.

Crisp Topping

1 1/2 cups	Flour	375 ml
1/2 cup	Corn starch	125 ml
1 1/2 cups	Rolled oats	375 ml
1 1/2 cups	Brown sugar	375 ml
3/4 cup	Melted butter	175 ml

Mix together until crumbly.

Substitutions: Apples may be used instead of the blueberries if preferred.

Chee Chu, Chef
Turtle Creek Café

Lemon Curd and Saskatoon Berry Ice Cream Profiteroles
with Whiskey and Chocolate Fondue

Serves: 10

Lemon Curd and Saskatoon Berry Ice Cream

Yields: 4 cups (1 litre)

8	Lemons	8
8	Eggs	8
3/4 lb.	Sugar (about 1 1/2 cups)	350 g
3/4 lb.	Butter	350 g
4 1/3 cups	Plain vanilla ice cream	1 litre
1/2 cup	Saskatoon berries	125 ml

Juice the lemons and strain. Mix the eggs and sugar together then add the lemon juice. Set up a double boiler and then cook on medium heat for about 1 hour, stirring on occasion. Once the mixture is thick, take off the heat and place in an ice bath. Whisk in your butter then let cool. Blend in half of the lemon curd and 1/2 cup (125 ml) of Saskatoon berries into the ice cream and refreeze. You can store the remaining lemon curd in the refrigerator for up to 2 weeks.

Profiteroles (Pâté à Choux)

8 2/3 cups	Milk	2 litres
1 lb.	Butter	450 g
1/2 oz.	Salt	15 g
6 cups	Bread flour	700 g
24	Eggs	24

Bring milk, butter and salt to a rolling boil. Combine flour with liquid until the mixture is smooth and rolls free from the side of the pot. Remove from heat and slowly add eggs until a medium stiff paste is obtained. Blend well after each addition of eggs. Pipe on a baking sheet in small rosettes and bake at 400° F (200° C) for a good half hour.

Alberta Springs Whiskey and
Milk Chocolate Fondue

1 lb.	Milk chocolate	450 g
1/4 cup	Heavy cream (35%), hot	50 ml
2 oz.	Alberta Springs Whiskey, warmed	50 ml

Melt the chocolate in a double boiler. When the chocolate is melted, add the hot cream with heated whiskey and blend together.

Assembly: Scoop a small spoonful of the ice cream into a sliced profiterole. Drizzle the whiskey and chocolate fondue sauce over the profiterole.

Roary MacPherson C.C.C., Executive Chef
The Fairmont Hotel Macdonald

Chestnut Tirami Su

Serves: 6

4 oz.	Mascarpone	125 g
4 oz.	Chestnut purée	125 g
4	Egg yolks	4
1/2 cup	**or** Crème Anglaise (see below)	125 ml
3 oz.	Sugar	75 g
1/4 cup	Whipping cream	60 ml
4	Egg whites	4
3	Gelatin sheets	3
2 oz.	Kirsch	60 ml
7 oz.	Bing cherries, canned (reserve juice)	200 g
1/2 cup	Syrup	100 ml
1 pack	Ladyfinger biscuits	1 pack
	Cacao powder **or** chocolate shavings for garnish	

Mix mascarpone and chestnut purée together. Add the yolks beaten with one third of the sugar or use Crème Anglaise. Mix in gelatin, dissolved in two thirds of the Kirsch. Fold in cream and then the whipped egg whites, beaten with two thirds of the sugar, last. Spread half of creamy mixture in bottom of glass or ceramic loaf pan 5 x 10 inches (12 x 25 cm). Mix one third of Kirsch with syrup and reserved cherry juice. Dip Ladyfingers into syrup mixture and cover first layer of cheese mixture. Place cherries over biscuits. Spread remaining cream over top and sprinkle with cacao powder or chocolate shavings. Refrigerate for 6 to 8 hours before serving.

Crème Anglaise

1 cup	Milk	250 ml
3	Egg yolks	3
2 oz.	Vanilla sugar	50 g

Mix egg yolks and sugar well together. In a saucepan, scald milk over medium heat and very slowly stir into egg-yolk mixture. Place back on stove and carefully reheat stirring until sauce coats the back of a wooden spoon. Remove quickly and strain. Cool using a hand whisk to beat the mixture strongly.

Peter Johner, Owner/Chef
Packrat Louie Kitchen & Bar

Crêpe Suzette

Yields: 12 crêpes

1	Egg	1
2 cups	Milk	500 ml
1/8 tsp.	Vanilla extract	0.5 ml
1 1/2 cup	Flour	375 ml

Mix eggs, milk and vanilla. Whisk in small amounts of flour at a time until the batter is smooth. Heat a non-stick saucepan on medium heat and spray with cooking oil. Add 2 oz. (55 ml) of batter to the pan as you tilt the pan in a circular motion to evenly distribute the crêpe batter. Cook on one side if you are going to serve them right away and lightly on the second side as well, if you are preparing them ahead of time. Repeat until all the batter is used.

Suzette Sauce

1/2 cup	Sugar	125 ml
1/2 tsp.	Butter	2 ml
1/2 oz.	Grand Marnier liqueur	15 ml
1/2 cup	Fresh orange juice	125 ml
1	Orange, zest	1

Heat the sugar and butter until they have almost caramelized. Flambé with Grand Marnier, paying careful attention to the flame. Add orange juice and reduce until it becomes syrup.

Serving suggestion: Roll crêpe with whipped cream, garnish with zest of an orange and peeled orange slices. Pour sauce over rolled crêpe and orange slices.

Mike Day, Chef
Three Muskateers

White Chocolate Lemon Tarts

Serves: 6

6	Prebaked tart shells, 5 inch (12 cm)	6
1 cup	Heavy cream (35%)	250 ml
3	Eggs	3
1/4 cup	Sugar	50 ml
3/4 cup	Fresh lemon juice	175 ml
6 tbsp.	Butter	90 ml
3/4 cup	White chocolate chips	175 ml
2 tsp.	Vanilla extract	10 ml

Whip cream to medium peak and set aside. Whisk the eggs together with the sugar. Add the lemon juice and butter to the egg and sugar mixture and cook on low heat, stirring constantly until the mixture begins to thicken. Remove the pot from the stove and stir in the white chocolate until it has melted, then add the vanilla extract. Let the mixture cool on the counter until luke warm, then fold in the whipped cream. Spoon the mixture into the tart shells and refrigerate for 1 hour.

Serving suggestion: Serve with fresh seasonal berries and a sprig of fresh mint.

Darrell Russell, Pastry Chef
Café de Ville

Chocolate Pecan Spring Rolls with Ginger Syrup

Serves: 2

2	Spring roll wrapper, 8 inch (20 cm) square	2
10	Pecans	10
10	Chocolate chips	10
	All purpose flour and water mixture	
	Cooking oil for deep frying	

Put a single wrapper on a flat surface. Brush flour and water mixture along the outside edges of the wrapper. Place 5 pecans and 5 chocolate chips in a diagonal line from one corner of the wrapper to the opposite corner. Fold the right corner over the pecans and onto the left side. Roll the wrap to assume a spring roll shape, remembering to fold in the ends to make a neat package. Deep fry for 5 minutes.

Ginger Syrup

1/2 cup	Brown sugar	125 ml
1 tbsp.	White sugar	15 ml
1 tbsp.	Ginger, ground	15 ml
1 tsp.	Cinnamon	5 ml
1 tsp.	Fresh lemon juice	5 ml

Cook the sugar with the spices over medium heat until it turns into a syrup. Pour over the roll.

Tanya, Chef
Lemongrass Café

Callebaut Chocolate Mousse Benedictine

Serves: 4-6

Mousse

7 oz.	Dark chocolate couverture (Callebaut recommended)	200g
3 tbsp.	Strong coffee	45 ml
3 oz.	Benedictine	85 ml
5	Egg yolks	5
3 oz.	Sugar	80 g
5	Egg whites	5
1/2 cup	Whipping cream, for garnish	125 ml

Break chocolate into small pieces and melt in a double boiler. Take off burner and leave warming. Add coffee and Benedictine. Whisk egg yolks and 1oz. (30 g) of sugar until sugar is completely dissolved. Mix egg yolks with the melted chocolate. Whisk egg whites and 2 oz. (50 g) of sugar until firm peaks are formed. Fold egg white mixture into the chocolate mix. Chill in refrigerator 2 to 3 hours before serving.

Cookie

5	Phyllo pastry sheets	5
1/2 cup	Butter, melted	125 ml
10 tbsp.	Sugar	150 ml

Put a phyllo pastry sheet on counter and brush with butter. Evenly sprinkle 2 tbsp. (30 ml) of sugar on top. Place second layer of pastry on top and repeat process until all layers are used. Place an even weight on top and refrigerate for half an hour. Cut into desired shapes and bake in a preheated 400° F (200° C) oven for 2 to 3 minutes or until golden brown. Check often. Allow to cool.

Assembly: Place one phyllo cookie on a plate, add one scoop of mousse and repeat process. Garnish with whipping cream.

Serving suggestion: Lorraine Ellis and Sabrina Warnholz, our wine stewards, recommend a Hennessey XO brandy.

Cyrilles Koppert, Proprietor
Manor Café

Millefeuille
with Fresh Berries

Serves: 4

10 oz.	Puff pastry, cut into 2 squares	300 g
1 cup	Whipping cream	250 ml
4 tsp.	Raspberry jam	20 ml
a few drops	Vanilla extract	a few drops
	Icing sugar	
	Seasonal berries	

Preheat the oven to 375° F (190° C). Roll out the pastry dough very thinly. You can use a pasta machine set to second finest (2 mm) setting. Roll until you obtain two rectangular strips. Place on a cookie sheet and bake in the oven for 8 to 10 minutes. Let cool.

Whip the cream until firm, add vanilla and icing sugar to your liking.

Assembly: Cut the puff pastry into 8 pieces, 1 1/2 inches (4 cm) wide. Spread 1 tsp. (5 ml) of raspberry jam on four of the pieces. Cover with a spoonful of whipped cream. Place some berries in the cream, then cover the top with a plain piece of puff pastry. Dust with icing sugar.

Serving suggestion: We usually serve this dessert with vanilla custard cream and raspberry coulis. Bon Appetit!

Eric Plantier, Executive Chef
Plantier's

Banana and Kahlua Bread Pudding

Yields: 1 loaf

1 loaf	Sweet bread or white bread, diced	1 loaf
2/3 cup	Heavy cream (35%)	150 ml
3 1/2 oz.	Brown sugar	100 g
1 oz.	Honey	30 ml
4 tsp.	Banana syrup	20 ml
4 tsp.	Kahlua	20 ml
2	Eggs	2
2 oz.	Pecans	50 g
2	Bananas, sliced	2
	Butter, to coat pan	

Mix the cream, brown sugar, honey, banana syrup, Kahlua and eggs in a large bowl until combined. Add diced bread, pecans and sliced bananas. Mix until combined and allow to rest for 30 minutes. But-ter the inside of a non-stick loaf pan. Pour the bread mixture into the pan — pushing it down a little. Place the loaf in a preheated oven at 425° F (220° C) and bake for 12 minutes.

Kahlua Sauce

1 cup	Cream (35%)	250 ml
1 oz.	Sugar	30 g
4 tsp.	Kahlua	20 ml
1/4	Vanilla bean	1/4
3	Egg yolks	3

In a small pot, combine cream, sugar, Kahlua and vanilla bean. Bring to a simmer on medium heat. In a medium bowl add egg yolks. Remove the bean. Begin whisking and slowly add the hot cream, a little at first, then the rest while you keep whisking. Strain the mixture into a bowl and allow to cool.

Pour over the bread pudding before serving.

Caramel Sauce

5 oz.	Sugar	150 g
1/4 cup	Water	50 ml
4 tsp.	Butter	20 g
4 tsp.	Cream	20 ml

In a small pot, combine sugar and water. Over high heat allow it to boil until it turns a golden brown. Remove from heat, add butter and cream, stirring until combined. Pour over the bread pudding and Kahlua sauce.

Shonn Oborowsky, Executive Chef
Characters

Passion for Chocolate
with Grand Marnier Sabayon

Serves: 10

1 tbsp.	Butter	15 ml
1/4 cup	Cocoa powder	50 ml
4.5 oz.	Milk chocolate	130 g
4.5 oz.	Bittersweet chocolate	130 g
1/2 cup	Butter, cubed small	125 ml
5	Egg yolks	5
6	Eggs	6
3/4 cup	Sugar	175 ml
4 tbsp.	Triple Sec	50 ml
1/2 cup	Flour	125 ml

Butter 10 ramekins and dust with cocoa powder. Melt milk and bittersweet chocolate with butter. In a mixing bowl place egg yolks, eggs, sugar, and Triple Sec and whip in a water bath to bring eggs to room temperature. Place in mixer stand and using a whip attachment, whip on medium speed until pale in colour, approximately 5 minutes. Reduce speed to low. Gradually add flour until it is well incorporated. Add chocolate mixture and beat at medium-low speed for a further 5 minutes. Pour into prepared ramekins until threequarters full and bake for 7 minutes at 350° F (180° C).

Serving suggestion: When ready to serve, reheat until tops puff up high. Invert onto plate and serve with sabayon sauce.

Sabayon Sauce

6	Egg yolks	6
6 oz.	Granulated sugar	170 g
1 cup	Grand Marnier	250 ml

Beat the egg yolks and sugar in a stainless steel bowl until light and fluffy. Add Grand Marnier. Place over simmering water and continue to whip constantly until the mixture is hot and thick enough to coat a spoon. Serve hot as soon as possible.

Patrizio Sacchetto, Master Chef
Via Vai

Coeurs à la Crème

Yields: 12 small moulds

12 oz.	Cream cheese, softened	375 g
8 oz.	Sour cream, low fat	250 g
3 tbsp.	Icing sugar	45 ml
1/2 tsp.	Vanilla flavour	2 ml
1/2 tsp.	Fresh lemon juice	2 ml
pinch	Salt	pinch

You will need some special equipment: Coeurs à la Crème moulds and a package of cheesecloth.

Using an electric mixer beat ingredients together for 8 to 10 minutes, or until smooth. Force mixture through a fine sieve into a bowl to remove any lumps. Line moulds with a single layer of damp cheesecloth and divide cheese mixture among moulds, smoothing tops. Tap the mould lightly on countertop to help the mixture settle. Fold overhanging cheesecloth over the tops of the moulds.

Place moulds in a shallow baking dish to catch any drips and refrigerate for at least 4 hours, preferably overnight. The coeurs can be made up to 2 days in advance if kept refrigerated. Unmold moulds, and carefully peel off cheesecloth. Let stand at room temperature for 20 minutes before serving.

Serving suggestion: This is a traditional French dessert which tastes great with fresh berries, berry sauce or, in a pinch, jam. Spoon topping around coeurs to serve.

Darcy Radies, Chef
The Blue Pear

Ukrainian Honey Cake

Serves: 20

1 cup	Liquid buckwheat honey	250 ml
1/2 cup	Soft butter	125 ml
1 cup	Packed brown sugar	250 ml
4	Eggs, separated	4
2 1/2 cups	All purpose flour	625 ml
1 tsp.	Baking soda	5 ml
1 tsp.	Baking powder	5 ml
1/2 tsp.	Salt	2 ml
1 tsp.	Cinnamon	5 ml
pinch	Cloves, ground	pinch
1 cup	Walnuts, finely chopped	250 ml
1 cup	Sour cream	250 ml

Preheat oven to 325° F (160° C)

Heat honey to a boil if it is not already in a liquid state. Cool to room temperature. Beat butter with half of the sugar. Beat in egg yolks, one at a time. Add honey. Stir in sifted dry ingredients and nuts alternately with the sour cream. Beat egg whites until fluffy and then beat in remaining sugar. Beat until stiff and moist. Fold into honey batter. Spread evenly in a greased, deep, round spring-form pan or tube pan. Bake for 50 minutes, then lower heat to 300° F (150° C) and bake until centre is set, about 25 more minutes. Cool.

Serving suggestion: Serve with whipped cream and fresh fruit.

Marge Choma, Chef/Owner
The Pyrogy House, The Pyrogy House Cook Book

Half Hour Pudding – A Traditional Prairie Recipe

Serves: 12

3/4 cup	Brown sugar	175 ml
2 tbsp.	Butter	30 ml
1 cup	Hot water	250 ml
2 tsp.	Salt	10 ml
1 tsp.	Vanilla	5 ml
11/2 cup	Fruit e.g. raisins, apricots etc	375 ml

Mix and bring to a boil brown sugar, butter, hot water, salt and vanilla. Add fruit, simmer for 5 minutes. Pour into a cake pan.

3/4 cup	Brown sugar	175 ml
2 tbsp.	Butter	30 ml
1 cup	Flour	250 ml
2 tsp.	Baking powder	30 ml
1/2 cup	Milk	125 ml
1 tsp.	Vanilla	5 ml

Mix all ingredients together and spoon on top of first part. Bake until cake turns brown at 350° F (180° C) for about 40 minutes.

Marge Choma, Chef/Owner
The Pyrogy House, The Pyrogy House Cook Book

125

Bittersweet Chocolate Cake
with Custard Sauce

Serves: 8

1 lb.	Bittersweet chocolate, chopped	500 g
2 cups	Butter, unsalted	500 ml
1 3/4 cups	Sugar	400 ml
10	Eggs, room temperature, separated	10
1 tsp.	Grand Marnier or orange liqueur	5 ml
1 tsp.	Vanilla extract	5 ml

Butter and flour a 12-inch spring-form pan; shake out excess flour. Place rack in middle of oven and preheat to 250° F (130° C). Combine chocolate and butter in heavy 3 quart (3 litre) saucepan. Stir until melted over medium heat, cool to room temperature, stirring occasionally. In a large bowl, combine 11/2 cups (375 ml) sugar with egg yolks. Beat on medium speed until mixture is light, fluffy and lemon-coloured, 8 to 10 minutes. Blend in cooled chocolate. Set aside. In a medium bowl, beat egg whites until soft peaks form. Beat in remaining 1/4 cup (50 ml) sugar, liqueur and vanilla until medium stiff peaks form. Using a rubber spatula, fold one quarter of beaten egg whites into chocolate mixture to lighten it. Fold in remaining whites. Pour batter into prepared pan. Bake until wooden pick inserted in centre comes out clean, approximately 3 hours. Cool in pan on wire rack for 15 minutes. Remove side of pan and cool completely. Remove bottom of pan, invert cake onto a serving plate. Chill.

Serving suggestion: Serve with fresh fruit, custard sauce, or preserved fruits (brandied cherries) and/or whipped cream.

Custard Sauce

2 cups	Milk	500 ml
1	Egg, large	1
2	Egg yolks, large	2
1/3 cup	Sugar	75 ml
2 tbsp.	Orange flavoured liqueur	30 ml
1 tsp.	Vanilla extract	5 ml

Scald milk in top of double boiler. Mix eggs and sugar together. Add milk and stir over simmering water in a double boiler until custard coats a metal spoon; about 10 to 15 minutes. Add liqueur and vanilla. Cover, chill.

Dennis Vermette, Executive Chef
Louisiana Purchase Restaurant

Restaurants

Café Select

The eclectic Select is all about balancing mood, service, and deft cuisine. All of which are guaranteed to add up to a fine evening out. This mainstay in the Edmonton restaurant scene opened in the summer of 1984 with a household electric stove and a shoestring budget. The menu presents a blend of traditional and contemporary cuisine; paying homage to the past in a manner that can be valued in the present. This intimate and atmospheric dining room where dark wood dominates, seats 90 patrons and has a reasonably priced, well-selected wine list. The service is deferential and professional. A local favourite with a full menu served until 2:00am everyday.

Mon-Fri 11:30-2:00am • Sat-Sun, 5:00pm-2:00am • 10018-106 Street, Edmonton, AB • 423-0419

Khazana Restaurant

Although the seasons and menus change, Khazana remains sheltered at the heart of Edmonton. In snow, in rain, in steaming heat, the restaurant shares its awesome "indiabonafide" cuisine and the best hospitality for an intimate luncheon or for a glowing evening of fine dining. Khazana cultivates the loyalty of their customers by listening and anticipating their needs and wants. Their classic menu includes Machhli Kebab, lovingly marinated salmon with freshly ground spices and grilled to mouth-watering perfection. Also featured on the menu are: Jhinga Vindaloo, garam masala at its best; Murgh Malaiplump, breast of chicken flavoured in a velvety cream sauce and grilled in clay ovens; and Peshwari Kebab, diced cubes of lamb seasoned in a blend of flavours and roasted tandoori fashion. Visit the web site at www.khazana.ab.ca

Mon-Thurs 11:30am-2:30pm, 5:00pm-10:00pm • Fri 11:30am-2:30pm, 5:00pm-11:00pm • Sat 5:00pm-11:00pm • Sun 5:00pm-10:00pm • 10177-107 Street • 702-0330

La Ronde, Chateau Lacombe

Specializing in Albertan Cuisine, the beef, bison and buffalo are carefully prepared with expertise by Chef Jasmin. Along with an outstanding meal, you can watch the Edmonton skyline unfold as La Ronde, the first revolving restaurant in the province, gives you the whole picture as you dine in comfort. One revolution takes 90 minutes, just the right encouragement to slow down and enjoy the evening! Click on the web site at www.chateaulacombe.com

Mon-Sun 5:30pm-11:00pm • Sunday brunch 10:30am-2:00pm • 10111 Bellamy Hill • 428-6611

Lemongrass Café

Located in the southern part of Edmonton, the Lemongrass Café is a fresh creative Vietnamese café offering traditional specialties such as lemongrass chicken or salmon served in banana leaves with ten spices. Garnering rave reviews and word of mouth recommendations, the café is comfortable and airy with a stylish interior. It is well worth a visit.

Mon-Fri 11:00am-2:00pm • Tues-Sun 5:00pm-9:30pm • 10417 51 Avenue NW N • 413-0088

Louisiana Purchase Restaurant

Chef Dennis Vermette and his Sous-chefs, including Russ Paranich, creatively dazzle Edmonton diners with their tasty Cajun and Creole cuisine. A fun and lively restaurant, Louisiana Purchase Restaurant creates fabulous seafood classics and creative Louisiana fare. There is something for everyone on the menu and it will take a few visits to sample it all. Gatherings large and small will be comfortable and welcomed.

Mon-Thurs 11:30am-10:00pm • Fri 11:30am-11:00pm • Sat 5:00pm-11:00pm • Sun 4:30pm-9:30pm • 10320-111 Street • 420-6779

Normand's

Normand's is a cozy little Bistro with a relaxed atmosphere where your hosts Lezlie and Normand Campbell will welcome you personally at the door. Each day you can look forward to a new lunch feature including soup, sandwich and fresh fish. The dinner menu is fine regional cuisine with a French accent. Here you will find at least one wild game dish each night and exquisitely prepared sauces which compliment each and every dish. Normand and his executive chef Cui are the creative inspiration behind this Edmonton gem. Visit Normand, Lezlie and Cui at www.normands.com.

Mon-Fri 11:30am-3:00pm • Sun-Thurs, 5:00pm-10:00pm • Fri and Sat 5:00pm-11:00pm • 11639 Jasper Avenue • 482-2600

The Blue Pear

The Blue Pear Restaurant, owned and operated by Chef Darcy Radies and his wife Jessie, is an intimate restaurant that can seat 35 people comfortably. Reservations are highly recommended. They offer a 5-course, *prix fixe* menu of classically inspired dishes with a modern twist. The menu changes every month to allow Darcy to take advantage of seasonal items and local specialties. Darcy and Jessie support local growers and producers and believe that great food starts with great ingredients. You will find a variety of local products on the menu throughout the year ranging from locally smoked salmon to locally grown organic vegetables and regional cheeses. You are encouraged to take your time, savour and enjoy your meal fully. To see the current menu or to make reservations, log on to www.thebluepear.com.

Wed-Sat 6:00pm-10:00pm • 10634 - 123 Street • 482-7178

Plantier's Restaurant

Traditional elegance combined with classic French cuisine distinguished Eric Plantier's restaurant. A landmark restaurant on the Edmonton scene for many years, Plantier's set a standard in the city for fine dining. Having recently closed the restaurant, Eric has moved on. Included in this book are a few of his signature dishes.

Polos Café

A fabulously gifted chef, award winning Judy Wu is the culinary wizard behind the kitchen door at the Polos Café. Start with the interesting décor and the warm welcome at the door from Wilson, Judy's brother and you will right away be prepped to savour and delight in the creative and colourful menu. A fusion of Chinese and Italian or of east and west, the menu is as familiarly unfamiliar and original as they come. Currently relocating, call 432-1371 for updated information. When their new location has been decided, it will be posted on Altitude's web site at www.altitudepublishing.com.

The Copper Pot Restaurant

A relatively new seafood restaurant in Edmonton, The Copper Pot is downtown offering convenience, delicious cuisine and a river valley view, which includes the legislature and the Highlevel Bridge! Specialties are offered daily at both lunch and diner and the seafood is always cooked to perfection! A partnership between Normand (of Normand's) and Simon has given Edmonton diners a creative and refreshing new menu. Visit us to find out more about the restaurant at www.copperpot.ca

Mon-Thurs 11:30am-10:00pm • Fri and Sat 11:30am-11:00pm • Closed Sunday • 9707-110 Street • 452-7800

Via Vai

Gourmet Magazine said Chef Sacchetto "demonstrates eloquently the range of his prodigious gifts as a creative Italian chef and combines masterful techniques with the sensibility of an artist". Master Chef Patrizio Sacchetto was voted one of the top 10 chefs of America by the New York Times American Gold Medal Certification. He brought his culinary expertise to Edmonton and garnered a loyal following at Via Vai Restaurant. At Via Vai, all the ingredients for a truly exemplary dining experience came together in a delectable profusion of sights, sounds, aromas and, of course, tastes. Currently closed and planning to relocate, call 780-486-5802 for information. When their new location has been decided, it will be posted on Altitude's web site at www.altitudepublishing.com.

Three Muskateers

When you enter this crêperie you will feel like you have just walked onto the set of La Bohème or onto the streets of Paris in the late 19th century! Colourfully decorated with paintings and murals, the Three Muskateers offers an amazing selection of savory

and sweet gourmet crêpes and other French fare. The highly-lauded crêpe house is the creative effort of Christoph Mathieu, who with Chef Mike Day, has succeeded in bringing a touch of French life to this western city.

Mon-Fri 11:30am-10:00pm • Sat-Sun 10:00am-11:00pm • 10416 82 Ave • 437-4239

The Pyrogy House

An Edmonton institution, The Pyrogy House, has been serving Edmonton diners for 36 years, dishing up the most fabulous home made Ukrainian food you'll ever taste. The restaurant has a dining room as well as offering take out and is easily identified for the first time visitor by its colourful mural which covers the exterior of the restaurant. Ten different kinds of pyrogies can be found daily on the menu along with traditional delights such as honey cake, sour-croute soup and other family recipes. Owner Marge Choma, found in the kitchen on most days, and her husband Robert are third-generation Ukrainian Canadians and remember being served many of the same meals when they were growing up. The Pyrogy House welcomes you to come and enjoy some of Edmonton's culinary heritage.

Mon-Thurs 11:30am-9:00pm • Fri 11:30am-9:45pm • Sat 4pm-9:45pm • Sun 4:00pm-8:45pm • 12510 – 118 Avenue NW • 454-7880

Café de Ville

Casual fine dining in the heart of beautiful 124th Street just north of Jasper Avenue and the river valley. Step into Café de Ville and feel the elegant warmth of the room with its cozy fireplace and smooth jazz playing overhead or enjoy our picturesque patio. Our relaxed atmosphere and knowledgeable service offers a perfect setting for any occasion. Chef Paul

Campbell and his team of certified chefs will please your palate with their creative and innovative cuisine. Pastry Chef, Darrell Russell, will complete your dining experience with one of his sinful delights. The owners, Jane Pawson-Loblaw and Anita and Mark Lewis, welcome you to their restaurant and your home away from home. Menu items: House-smoked Atlantic Salmon Appetizer, wide variety of signature pastas, Dijon Crusted Rack of Lamb, Alberta Pork Tenderloin and Rocky Mountain Venison. Please visit us at www.cafedeville.com for updated info.

Mon-Thu 11:30am-10pm • Fri-Sat 11:30am-12am • Sun 10am-2pm, 5pm-10pm • 10137-124 St. • 488-9188

Characters

The menu at Characters often abounds with a pastiche of tempting dishes in the styles of Canadian continental, Asian, or French cooking, the roots of each – as well as some of the ingredients – are usually in the North American genre. With seasonal variations, a single meal for instance a diner, might enjoy a Pan-seared Duck Breast, Rack of Lamb, Beef Tenderloin (wrapped with bacon, goat cheese and foie gras with Madeira wine sauce) and a Fillet Venison (baked in puff pastry with wild mushrooms, Brussels sprouts and raspberry jus). Dessert could be served at your table of choice or by the fire on the comfortable oversized couches. Some desserts of choice may be a Crème Brûlée, Mango Cheesecake or a seasonal soufflé. The charisma of the Chef contributes greatly to the warmth of the renovated warehouse, with exposed brick of the 85-seat main dining room. Another addition of the 20-seat private party room satisfies the customer hosting a special event. At a sassy semicircular food bar, an additional eight or so lucky diners can watch Chef Shonn personally create magic for them as he turns culinary excitement out of his skillets, all the while chatting with his audience and wowing them with his twinkly, puckish grin, that's his character. For more information log on to www.characters.ca

Lunch Mon-Fri 11-2 • Dinner Tue-Sat 5:30-10:30 • 10257-105 St. • 425-1550

Donna at the Citadel

Donna manages to translate big city ambience into a completely Edmonton friendly take on dramatic design and urbanity. Don't be afraid to order outside of your comfort zone. The menu offers an original deft take on world fusion cuisine with Rock Shrimp Cake, Rare Tuna Spring Rolls, Salmon in Chili Sauce, Nine Spice Roast Lamb or Peking Duck Salad. Modern beats sound throughout the space, flowers abound throughout the summer and a large common table in the beautiful martini bar puts cast, crew and clientele elbow to elbow après show. Located inside Edmonton's Citadel Theatre and in the heart of the Arts district.

Mon 11:30am-2pm • Tue-Fri 11:30am-11:30pm • Sat-Sun 5pm-11:30pm • 10177 – 99 St. • 429-3338

EastBound Eatery

EastBound is Edmonton's newest hot spot for Japanese Cuisine with a modern twist. We offer the freshest sushi, sashimi, tempura, as well as western steak and seafood with Oriental flavours. Our cooking philosophy is to make the food, so that you can enjoy every day. We stock many kinds of Japanese sake. We also offer takeout dinner boxes for your busy days, when you don't want to cook at home.

Mon-Thu 11:30am-10:30pm • Fri-Sat 11:30am-midnight • Sun 4:30-8:30pm • 11248-104 Ave. • 409-9027

Hardware Grill

Hardware Grill opened in 1996 in Edmonton's historic Goodridge Block. This upscale restaurant that once housed Edmonton's best-known hardware store, the W.W. Arcade, has now become a city mainstay for excellent food, outstanding service and warm ambiance. The grand room that once featured hammers, paint, nuts and bolts now invites you with warm earthy tones, brick paint, plum hardwood floors, impressive river valley views and spacious elegance. Hardware Grill is renowned for its seasonally inspired Canadian Prairie cooking and international award-winning wine list of over 500 selections. Owners Larry and Melinda Stewart are always there to attend to every detail of your dining experience, both lunch and dinner. The Wine Spectator has awarded Hardware Grill its "Award of Excellence" for their outstanding wine list 1997 through 2001. Hardware Grill has also been voted Where Magazine's Readers "Best Fine Dining" for 1998 – 2001, Enroute Magazine Readers 1998 "top 100 restaurants in Canada", and is listed in Anne Hardy's Where to Eat in Canada for 1998 – 2002, with a two star rating in 2001/2002. We are pleased to provide a smoke-free dining experience. For menu items and other information, please visit us at www.hardwaregrill.com.

Mon-Fri 11:30am-2pm • Mon-Sat 5-11 • Closed Sundays and Holidays • 9698 Jasper Ave. • 423-0906

Highlevel Diner

The most fantastic view of nighttime Edmonton can be seen at one of the city's coziest restaurants, the Highlevel Diner. Warm, enveloping and welcoming the Highlevel Diner's candlelit tables accent the eclectic art pieces on the walls and antique furniture throughout. The summertime patio is a great way to relax and enjoy a fruit frappa or Big Rock Ale on tap. Our international menu caters to a wide variety of palates, with fresh hearty and healthy foods. Our chef creates exciting soups and specials daily, as well as a different, fabulous salmon dish. Sunday night is our traditional prime rib dinner. Our legendary breakfast menu includes the Highlevel Diner's famous cinnamon buns, muffins and hot seven-grain cereal. A favourite community meeting spot for dinner, lunch or great coffee and desserts.

Mon-Thu 8am-11pm • Fri 8am-midnight • Sat 9am-midnight • Sun 9am-10pm • 10912 - 88 Ave. (southside of the HighLevel Bridge) • 433-0993 or 433-1317

Il Portico

This inviting downtown restaurant has long been a local favorite. A haven for those craving an exquisite meal with exceptional service, Il Portico boasts a vibrant atmosphere that's a little like being at a party where you are the guest of honor. Il Portico is a restaurant for the senses. Embrace the warmth and aroma from the open kitchen or slip downstairs for the "Big Night" feel of the private dining room. Whenever you go, Il Portico's lively menu is sure to impress. Using ingredients of the highest quality, Chef Kevin Lendrum's concoctions burst with the freshness that is the hallmark of Italian cuisine. And Il Portico's wine list boasts an impressive selection that allows you excellent pairing with every course, something you would expect from a six-time winner of the Wine Spectator Award of Excellence.

Mon-Fri 11:30 am – 11pm • Sat 5:30 – 11pm • Closed Sundays • 10012–107 St. N.W. • For reservations 424 – 0707 • portico@telusplanet.net

Union Bank Inn — Madison's Grill

Madison's Grill, located in the Historic Boutique Hotel the Union Bank Inn, offers regional Canadian cuisine with a Fusion Edge. The Chef, Brian Leadbetter and his team pride themselves in using fresh local & Alberta-made products. Their creative selections range from a Grilled Tenderloin Thai Salad Roll to Horseradish Crusted Fresh Salmon. This is complimented with a diverse wine selection, detailed customer service in an elegant setting, with soaring columns and a masonry fireplace. Private dining also available. Log on to www.unionbankinn.com

Mon-Thu 7am-10pm • Fri 7am-11pm • Sat 8am-11am & 5pm-11pm • Sun 8am-11am & 5pm-8pm • 10053 Jasper Ave. • 421-7171

Manor Café

The manor was the residence of former Alberta Attorney General John Farquar Lymburn (1926 to 1935), who built this lovely home in 1929. The integrity of the original structure has been maintained which allows for intimate dining, yet can accommodate private functions or corporate business dinners. At the Manor Café we strive to be one of Edmonton's best. Our focus is on product quality and service excellence. Our delicious desserts as well as our fresh baked breads are made "from scratch" on the premises. As part of our service every effort is made to accommodate modification to menu items due to special dining needs or preferences. For an online tour, please visit us at www.manorcafe.com

Mon-Sat 11am-11pm • Sun 5-10pm • 10109-125 Street • 482-7577

Packrat Louie Kitchen & Bar

Located in the heart of Old Strathcona, this Swiss-owned and operated bistro offers the finest quality of upscale fresh market cuisine. A favourite spot for the before and après-theatre crowd, Packrat Louie is right by the Varscona and Fringe Theatre Adventures. Among the tasty menu highlights are fresh fish, lamb shank, pasta, spätzle and weekly specials. Try the always popular assortment of wood oven pizzas, baked to perfection. You can choose from an award-winning wine list and to satisfy any sweet-tooth, Packrat Louie is also known for fine pastries and desserts like swiss chocolate truffles and pralines made on-site.

Tue-Sat 11:30am –11:30pm • 10335-83 Ave. • 433-0123

Pradera Café and Lounge — The Westin

Pradera Café and Lounge is located in the lobby of the Westin Edmonton, the leading provider of downtown hotel rooms and premium catered banquet space. Our menu in the three-meal Restaurant caters to a wide variety of customers, from our hometown fans to our traveling guests from abroad and from right here in our own beautiful province of Alberta. Our main food focus is regional Alberta cuisine, as our motto reflects; "Regional Inspired Cuisine with a Contemporary Flair". We have developed an excellent rapport with quite a number of local growers and purveyors of what we find to be some of the best products available in the world. On a daily basis we strive to include as many locally grown products as we can. www.thewestinedmonton.com

Mon-Fri 6:30am-11pm• Sat-Sun 7am-11pm • 10135, 100 Street • 426-3636

The Fairmont Hotel Macdonald — The Harvest Room

Located inside one of Edmonton's most famous landmarks, the Fairmont Hotel Macdonald, The Harvest Room is steeped in history and atmosphere. Be escorted inside this splendid Edwardian eatery by the top Maitre D' in the city of Edmonton, Brian Welsh and experience marble fixtures, chandelier lighting, vaulted windows and a patio that is second to none in the city, where people can enjoy a breathtaking view of the river valley. The Harvest Room offers regional Canadian cuisine, inspired by Executive Chef Roary MacPherson and his culinary team and by the abundance of fresh local ingredients that a province like Alberta has to offer. The Harvest Room is considered by many to be the top restaurant in the city and is ranked by J.D. Power Corporation as one of the top 5 restaurants in the Fairmont Hotel and Resort company. Click on www.fairmont.com

Breakfast, Mon-Fri 6:30 – 11am • Sat-Sun 7 – 11:30am • Lunch, Mon-Fri 11:30-2, Sat-Sun noon – 2pm • Dinner, Mon-Fri 5:30 – 10, Sat-Sun 5:30 - 9:00 • 10065-100 St. • Reservations 424-5181

Turtle Creek Café

Turtle Creek Café, a landmark nestled in the Old Strathcona and University communities, has been serving great food for over 14 years and is the choice destination for thousands of Edmontonians as well as diners from the surrounding municipalities. Enjoy an all day menu, suitable for anybody's tastes. Chef Chee Chu creates our wonderful "daily specials" that compliment the regular menu items. Owner Ian Boothe welcomes you to be pampered by his well-trained service staff, who offer the best in quality and satisfaction. Come join us at Turtle Creek Café, voted by Edmonton Entertainment Club Members as their "Favourite Restaurant" four years running. www.turtlecreek.ca

Mon-Thu 11:30am-10pm • Fri 11:30am-midnight • Sat 11am-11pm • Sun 11am-10pm • 8404-109 St. • 433-4202

Carole's Café and Frank's Place

For eight years, owner and chef Carole DeAngelis of Carole's Café in Edmonton's downtown has delighted patrons with her flair for cooking with flavour. Carole will soon be taking on a new challenge by joining her husband at his restaurant Frank's Place in Spruce Grove. The menu features time honoured Italian cuisine, using the freshest ingredients available. Frank's Place offers a comfortable and inviting atmosphere.

Mon-Fri 11:00am-2:00pm, 5:00pm-10:00pm • Sat & Sun 5:00pm-10:00pm • Sunday brunch • 304 Westgrove Drive • Reservations 962-5333

About the Editors

Myriam Leighton is a published writer who co-authored the original book in this series. She is an avid gardener and naturalist who like her co-author, Jennifer Stead, loves to experiment and be creative in her kitchen. Jennifer Stead is a professional artist and educator who gardens and cooks with pleasure.

Index

Tomato Tart, Roast, 38
Veal, Escallops Valle D'Auges, 19
Vegetable Terrine, Grilled, 40
Vinaigrette, Black Mustard Seed, 54
Vinaigrette, Cherry, 47
Vinaigrette, Ermite Bleu, 33
Vinaigrette, Orange and dill, 51
Vinaigrette, Raspberry Maple Dill, 60
Vinaigrette, Soya, 57
Vinaigrette, Sun-dried Tomato,
    Raspberry, 49

Risotto with Smoked Pancetta..., 86
Salmon, Marinated, Machhli
    Kebab, 84
Salmon, Seven Spices, Roasted..., 94
Salmon with Roasted Tomato
    Broth..., 82
Seafood Pasta, 70
Spaghetti Trastaverni, 73
Shrimp Piquante, 87
Trout, Yukon Gold Potato
    Risotto..., 74

Entrées

Bison Burger with Red Onion
    Marmalade..., 98
Bison, Lamb and Black Bean Chili, 68
Bison Meatloaf with Corn Cheddar
    Mash, 80
Bison Short Ribs, 78
Beef Tataki, 72
Beef Tenderloin topped with Tomato
    Basil Stew..., 62
Beef Tenderloin with Roasted Tomato
    Ancho Chili Sauce..., 67
Beef Wellington, 76
Black Bean Chili, 90
Bouillabaisse (Seafood Stew), 104
Chicken, Phyllo, 66
Chicken, Honey Gingered Teriyaki, 79
Chicken, Salt and Lemon Grilled, 77
Chicken, Select, 63
Chicken, Lemongrass, 99
Chicken, Savory Herb Roasted with
    Cranberry..., 69
Chili, Black Bean, 90
Chili, Lamb and Bison, 68
Halibut in Roasted Red and Green
    Pepper Sauces, 92
Lamb and Bison Chili, 68
Lamb, Encrusted Rack with
    Rosemary..., 89
Lamb, Rack with Grilled Potato and
    Eggplant Salad..., 64
Linguine Jambalaya, 106
Machhli Kebab, 84
Ostrich, Lemongrass-Spiced with Hot
    and Sour..., 100
Ostrich Steak with Cassis and
    Berries..., 88
Pork Tenderloin, BBQ Oriental, 71
Pyrogy Dough and Fillings, 96
Rabbit, Paddle River Organic with
    Smoked..., 91

Desserts

Banana and Kahlua Bread
    Pudding, 120
Blueberry Crisp, 111
Chocolate Cake, Bittersweet, 126
Chocolate Crème Brûlée, White, 108
Chocolate Lemon Tarts, White, 116
Chocolate Mousse Benedictine,
    Callebaut, 118
Chocolate Pecan Spring Rolls, 117
Chocolate with Grand Marnier
    Sabayon, 122
Coeurs à la Crème, 123
Crêpes Suzette, 115
Fondue, Whiskey and Milk
    Chocolate, 113
Half Hour Pudding, 125
Lemon Curd, 112
Millefeuille with fresh Berries, 119
Panna Cotta with Figs, Port, Honey
    and Lavender, 110
Profiteroles, Lemon Curd,
    Saskatoon..., 112
Soufflé, Pumpkin Spiced Rum and
    Cream Cheese, 109
Tirami Su, Chestnut, 114
Ukrainian Honey Cake, 124